Stepmotherhood

Stepmotherhood

HOW TO SURVIVE WITHOUT FEELING
FRUSTRATED, LEFT OUT, OR WICKED

CHERIE BURNS

THREE RIVERS PRESS • NEW YORK

Published by Three Rivers Press, New York, New York.
Member of the Crown Publishing Group.

Random House, Inc. New York, Toronto, London, Sydney, Auckland
www.randomhouse.com

THREE RIVERS PRESS is a registered trademark and the Three Rivers Press colophon
is a trademark of Random House, Inc.

Originally published in different form by Times Books in 1985.

Printed in the United States of America

Design by Susan Maksuta

Library of Congress Cataloging-in-Publication Data

Burns, Cherie.
    Stepmotherhood : how to survive without feeling frustrated, left out, or
    wicked / Cherie Burns—Rev. ed.
    Includes index.
    ISBN 0-609-80744-7(pbk.)
    1. Stepmothers—United States. 2. Stepfamilies—United States. I. Title.
HQ759.92.B86   2001
646.7'8—dc21   00-060776

ISBN 0-609-80744-7

10 9 8 7 6 5

To Hope and Anne,
my fellow initiates in
stepfamily life

Contents

With special thanks to Emily and John Visher, Clifford Sager, Thomas Seibt, Lillian Messinger, Teresa Adams, and the other family counselors who generously shared their time and expertise with me.

Introduction

The Art of Stepmotherhood

Stepmothering is an art, a survival technique, and an act of giving. It requires serious attention, careful thought, quick wit, and genuine involvement. Challenging, difficult, and usually worthwhile, it either licks you or you lick it.

Becoming a stepmother is a little bit like being a mail-order bride. The relationship ahead—what it will require and mean to you—is a mystery and a gamble. No matter what you envision, the reality is bound to be different. Stepmothering is even more unpredictable than natural mothering, which at least has built-in bonds. In stepmothering, you start from scratch.

At the heart of stepmothering is a simple

truth: you have joined a family. Granted, it's a different, untraditional, and loosely structured sort of family, but it is a family nonetheless. The consequences of that are far-reaching and significant. The "family" is a community of people who already function as a group. Other people's roles and attitudes are well established when you enter their midst. You are the new bride and initiate who must adapt and make your way, earn your place, and prove yourself. Needless to say, this is not what most of us have in mind when we get married.

When I first wrote *Stepmotherhood* I could not have predicted how relevant the subject would become during the next fifteen years. I understood that the number of stepmothers was likely to increase over time, but I didn't foresee that the role would become central to American family life. According to the Stepfamily Association of America, half of all Americans live in some variety of stepfamily situation and news reports proclaim that there are now 20 million stepfamilies in the United States. In seven years stepfamilies are expected to outnumber traditional families. With over 50 percent of first marriages ending in divorce, 65 percent of those involving children, and 75 percent of the divorced partners remarrying, it is plain to see that stepfamilies are here to stay and that more and more women are becoming stepmothers each year. There are approximately 15 million stepmothers in the United States today, according to recent estimates.

What has also become clear since I first wrote *Stepmotherhood* fifteen years ago is that stepmothering is an enduring and everchanging role for the women who assume it. I still maintain that stepmotherhood is a more emotionally gripping dilemma for new stepmothers than any other subgroup, but stepmotherhood's issues do not recede and go away over the years. As marriages, stepchildren, and, maybe most important, stepmothers themselves, change over time, the challenges in these relationships also shift and evolve. A stepmother who has existed in her stepfamily for ten years or more is likely to have learned that stepfamily issues do not disappear, but rather shift and reinvent themselves. Nothing stays the same for a stepmother any more than it does for biological mothers, and her role doesn't expire either.

Settling into early stepfamily relationships typically poses the most challenge and adjustment for any woman, but a stepmother's role is as permanent as her marriage. (And sometimes the relationships she shares with her husband's children continue even if the marriage ends.) For instance, early concerns about visitation schedules and household habits are likely to be supplanted later with issues over family reunions and stepgrandchildren. A stepmother is unlikely to find herself playing a stale role or creating a relationship that once mastered can be forgotten. The relationships between her and her husband and stepchildren are bound to keep changing—as is she—and reminding her that becoming a stepmother was and is a serious and continuing endeavor. The experiences of a stepmother in an older stepfamily (not necessarily an older stepmother) may be heartening to newer stepmothers who feel swamped by their problems but can look ahead to better times, so I've included them in a new chapter here. I now live in such a stepfamily, as do many of the women I interviewed originally. Most of us find stepfamily life easier these days.

The world we live in today is also a somewhat easier place for stepmothers. Schools are more accustomed and accommodating to stepfamily concerns. Even some greeting card companies have added lines that can be construed to include these special relationships. A stepmother can also find her peers online, and there are more local and national organizations of support groups for stepfamilies. There are also more women today who have experience in the role than at any time in history, so a stepmother need not look as far to find a model or a comrade. She need not feel like a pioneer or the oddity that she did a decade ago. What hasn't changed much is the private, emotional effect on her life. That continues to be what this book is about.

I didn't know it would be like this. I've said and heard that line so often that it is like a chant in my mind. It's uttered—or sobbed—by most stepmothers because it is impossible to anticipate what your relationship with your husband's children from another marriage will be like. The children approach you, their new stepmother, with their own combat wounds and family conditioning. Your husband, most likely, has never had to juggle the concerns of his children and his wife separately. If childless, you may never before have considered parenting, with its emotional demands, its diplomatic skills, and its link to your own psyche. In some cases, even your husband's ex-wife, though out of view, won't be out of mind if she plays a strong or controlling role with her children.

Any one of these complications is a factor to be reckoned with in new relationships, but a combination of two or more—the usual case for stepmothers—can make even strong women tremble. In combination with vacations, holidays, financial pressures, and daily tensions, they can become an emotional minefield.

I was twenty-six when I married and became the stepmother of two girls, ages sixteen and thirteen. I gave far more thought to marrying than I did to any sort of mothering, and I've since learned that women who marry divorced men with children usually begin that way. I thought I knew what I was getting into.

In my innocence, I figured that stepchildren came with the new arrangement, the way a garage comes with a new house.

There were the usual sticky problems of a second marriage: my husband's ex-wife, problems with visitation rights, etc., but I believed that once my husband and I were married, "the girls," as we called them, would renew a normal relationship with their father and accept me, even like me.

Seven years later when I began this book, I could see how unprepared I was for the series of difficult incidents and relationships that followed. I made adjustments and I grappled with my problem and discomforts mostly alone (although, my husband reminds me, not in silence). I didn't know anybody else in my position and I assumed that my stepmothering difficulties were unique. I was wrong.

I thought that stepmothers were an isolated corner of the population, like six-toed cats and people who still have their tonsils, until I began talking about the subject. To my surprise, whenever I mentioned stepmothering, it was a subject of keen interest in almost any company. We are in endless supply, and our need to know one another, to compare our experiences, and to share solutions is universal. Even the most private and reserved women open up when they learn that they are not the only one who faces a stepmothering problem. The topic is an icebreaker that cuts across all ages, professions, and social strata. Sometimes women I admired but hardly knew sought me out after they'd heard I was working on a book about stepmothers. "Does everybody have trouble with stepchildren? Would you like to hear about mine?" they would ask. Never before had I attracted such attention as a conversationalist.

The mere mention of thank-you notes, shared vacations, college costs, visiting stepchildren's bathroom habits—the list goes

on and on—invariably hits a nerve. Some of the most composed, mature, and effective women imaginable are dumbfounded to learn how "little things," such as the failure of a
stepchild to say goodbye or to look them in the face, can cata-
pult them into a fury or depression. Their own response to these
relatively insignificant acts challenges their secure self-image.
Fortunately, these reactions are understandable and frequently
humorous once a woman can step back far enough to see the
comedy in being brought to tears by a nine-year-old boy who
won't eat her mushroom sauce and forgets her birthday.

Each stepmothering situation has its own psychic potholes.
One woman, very "together" in every sense of the word, told me
how she suffers extreme anxiety when she waits for her husband
to pick her up after work. He also occasionally gives a lift to his
son, a young man in his twenties. "When the car comes in sight,
I wait to see if there are one or two heads inside. When there are
two, it's like having a stake driven into my chest. He puts a
damper on everything," she said. She is astonished at this reaction in herself. "It must sound so petty." Yet there are reasons
behind her feelings. Her stepson's attitude toward her is frosty.
When she returned to work after a week-long illness, he didn't
even acknowledge that she'd been absent or ill. "He just mum-
bled 'Hi' the way he always does," she noted.

Sometimes it's the subtle slights that hurt the most, that create the lingering impression that your stepchildren don't accept
you, that your gestures to them go unappreciated, or that you are
being awkward and tense in your role.

How you see yourself in your role is a common problem.
I know it well. I first experienced it when I accompanied my
sixteen-year-old stepdaughter to a rock concert. When she
introduced me to her friends as "my stepmother," my gut reac-

tion was, "Oh, no, that's not me!" But the incident started me thinking. After all, I *was* her stepmother. That was the word for me, so why should she have to say "my dad's wife," or use any other euphemism for our relationship? And what *did* this relationship mean?

This book attempts to answer that question—to discuss what being a stepmother means. It is not just a litany of woes and wrongs with which stepmothers must contend, though we often do have legitimate complaints. This book is intended to reexamine and to shed new light on stepmothering and its modern dimensions.

Though women would hardly rush to apply for stepmothering if an accurate job description appeared in the classifieds, the woman who attempts it is increasingly common. Schools, clubs, and summer camps now typically include information about both stepparents and natural parents on admission forms. Not only is a stepmother increasingly recognized as a presence in our society, but more important, nearly one third of all children under eighteen are personally affected by her success or failure in her role.

In much the same way that they unceremoniously arrive in her life, she lands in theirs. For better or for worse, she will affect their home life, their sense of family, life with their father, Christmases, birthdays, Bar Mitzvahs, and weddings from here on out. Her frequent appearance makes her more than just an odd adjunct to modern family life. She is an integral and important part of it, even if her stepchildren live with their mother.

Yet her importance is not necessarily accompanied by power or self-assurance. On the contrary, she may not know what she is about. She is often uncomfortable, uneasy, and full of feelings of inadequacy. Standing awkwardly on the threshold of her new family's life, she has no idea of how to enter gracefully. Sounds of family life that reach her both attract and alienate her. What right has she to interrupt, to ask for acceptance? she often asks. A family may not have been what she bargained for. *I didn't know it would be like this.*

Divorce and the suffering it causes to couples and their children have been widely examined during recent years. The latest reports assert that stepchildren have difficulty adjusting and are more likely to have academic and disciplinary problems than children who live with both biological parents. A stepmother should be aware of and concerned by this phenomenon, as most of those whom I've spoken with are. This book is not meant to belittle the hurt that occurs when a family breaks up. But to acknowledge those truths should not suggest that a stepmother lacks valid feelings and needs of her own. It is fair to expect a stepmother to be adult, to learn as she goes along, and to take responsibility for her involvement in the family she has married into. But divorced parents and children do not have a patent on frustrations and hurts.

Only in recent years have stepmothers gained professional advocates. The increasing number of family counselors who are stepmothers themselves is to some degree responsible for the shift. "If you haven't wrestled with this alligator [a stepfamily], it's not quite so easy to understand it," says Teresa Adams, a mother and a stepmother as well as a psychotherapist with a leading marriage counseling practice in New Orleans. "I'm not certain I could wholly empathize with stepfamilies' problems without the personal experience," says Adams.

When I first began investigating the library's literature on stepmothers, I was struck by the high expectations set for us in books and magazines. Some family counselors even advised us to subjugate ourselves to the needs of husbands and stepchildren because, it was reasoned, they had suffered the enormous loss of a nuclear family. The experience of the stepmother was often discussed in terms of giving aid and support to others. She was traditionally expected to perform like a miracle computer—strictly programmed for output—without feedback and input. In fact, her modern role is much more akin to interactivity since she is very much at the center of an entire network of family relations. Family professionals who understand her position now take the stepmother's point of view into account and acknowledge her importance.

Fortunately, the modern stepmother has a few things going for her. A real and deep commitment to and from a man who has learned a few things about himself and marriage in his previous experience is her best asset—even if he has clay feet regarding his children, as many fathers do. If in addition to a solid relationship with her husband she can put herself and her experience into focus by understanding stepmothering's peculiar chemistry and inherent obstacles, she can at least lift her own life to a happier plane. I hope this book will help stepmothers toward that goal.

This book is based on interviews with more than forty stepmothers who shared their stepmothering experience with me, and to whom I am especially grateful because I believe that their frankness has enabled me to write honestly about stepmothering.

As I took leave of most of those women, they often looked dubiously at me and said the same thing: "I hope you'll tell it like it really is." I vowed I would. One stepmother I know and respect was the most skeptical. She wondered if I would be able to discuss stepmothering honestly. "It's not always a happy story," she stated. I knew that painting an accurate picture of step-mothering would be a challenge,

I have tried to avoid glib reassurances and false cheeriness. The only lasting uplift to stepmothering comes after facing some sobering truths. There are solutions to many stepmothering problems, as the women who have arrived at them demonstrate, but sometimes a stepmother can't control all of the emotions of all the people involved. Sometimes her job is learning to live with the imperfections without letting them tear her apart. That's the real story about stepmothering. That's the way it really is.

Definitions

"You can't be a peer. You can't be a parent. It took me five years to figure it out."

"I was in our house looking out the window, watching the kids with my husband and his parents playing together on the lawn, and I thought: I don't like these people. I don't belong. My life rotated around them, always what was best for the children. How can you argue against that moral argument? But I resented it a lot."

As a stepmother, you are initially perceived, falsely or not, as a rival to the most traditionally revered and respected biological force in the family—the mother. If that's not enough to put some drama into your life, there's plenty more.

You are the last member to enter an extended family (the term most commonly used to describe these modern hybrids in which the natural parents are divorced and one or both are remarried), and you are often the last to grasp the significance of that. Family life is already in progress. You join it when you marry, at a time of high hopes, optimism, and a romantic view of family members, together with your commitment to them. Everyone else (your husband, his children, and their mother) is a bit more realistic. They know more about each other's strengths and weaknesses, moves and limits. The stepmother is an earnest newcomer—and not always a welcome one.

"Dad's new wife" has never ranked high on the roster of family endearments. No one has known exactly what to make of her, and she often shares their puzzlement. The trouble, as one psychologist points out, is that modern stepmothers typically lack the purpose they had in times past when a father was likely to remarry only after he was widowed, and his new wife moved in to rule the roost. Her role—to replace a natural mother—was crystal clear. Still, as Cinderella, Snow White, and a host of other plaintive young victims in children's stories remind us, the kids plainly loathed her. Trying to replace a natural mother was undoubtedly a terrible task. As we modern stepmothers also soon learn, trying *not* to replace her isn't a snap either.

Stepmothering is not simple in practice or in its effect. The role's lack of clarity and uncertainty can muddy your self-image and self-esteem. A stepmother goes from merely marrying a man with children to facing a myriad of psychological and emotional truths. It's a quick, short trip, and it leaves many of us feeling overwhelmed and out of touch with our own lives. Personal considerations seem small and unworthy against the larger issues of children, pain, and divorce.

What is a stepmother really? The *fact* of being a stepmother can be described accurately—she is married to a man who has children by somebody else—but the *meaning* is seldom examined. Current society doesn't even seem to have a standard for the role.

No wonder we stepmothers feel so ill at ease. There are no models, no precedents, no fantasy stepmums in television commercials to depict what an ideal stepmother should be. The only role model is a natural mom, and it is disastrous for us to emulate her. Even the greeting card industry, which has found ways to celebrate almost every conceivable relationship and occasion, dances around stepfamily relationships. Hallmark has introduced a new line devoted to nontraditional families but the word "step" is never used, which surely says something about society's unease with us.

Stepmothering means filling a new position in a family and creating a relationship to the children that is different from any either you or they have known before. For many women, one of the most disconcerting aspects of stepmotherhood is the title: stepmother. Those last two syllables are difficult for them—especially for women without children of their own—to feel at home with.

Changing an awkward title almost never works. Changing our understanding of what the term implies does help.

The stepmother's time has come. The rates of divorce and remarriage have swelled her number and dramatically changed her function, even if her public image still lags behind. The dusty old pinched and negative notion of stepmothering is going out of style as a quarter of a million modern women become new stepmothers every year and leave their imprint on the title. A stepmother is no longer an apologetic oddity on the fringe of family life. Instead, she has a full-fledged part in a new kind of family that is fashioned around new needs and relationships rather than an inapplicable old design of traditional family life. She is neither imitative of the natural mother nor a half member of a family as a helpful maiden aunt or kindly neighbor might be—old parallels that were formerly applied to her status.

Though the semantics of stepmotherhood can be off-putting, the term does describe a relationship to your husband's children. It is a term that is earning more respect as our number increases and our function comes to be appreciated as the glue that holds together families—past, present, and future.

Stepmothering will always have trials and tribulations that no amount of consciousness-raising or public regard can prevent. The persons involved determine the quality of any relationship, but a stepmother often underestimates the ready-made aspect of marrying a divorced man with children. She becomes a stepmother as well as a wife at the altar.

It's the original package deal—pick one, get one (or more) free. A six-month stepmother who feels that she didn't realize this fundamental law about stepmothering when she married, said, "It was as though I came along with just my overnight bag. I didn't know he had all these bags and suitcases waiting out in the car."

The same is often true of in-law relationships, but in the latter, convention dictates the primacy of husband and wife. All parties are adults, and it's considered proper that a son leave his mother and father to form a new household when he marries. That a father should make trade-offs between his children and his new wife, even though both have proper claims on him, is not so acceptable. If anything, public perception puts the needs and wishes of children, especially children of divorce, above a second wife's. Her uncertain rank in the family hierarchy becomes part of her frustration. Stepmotherhood is one of the most complex family roles a woman can undertake.

Stereotypes of stepmothering—the public's and our own—add to our difficulties and disappointment. Most of us enter stepmothering believing that we must love our stepchildren and be loved by them in return. The fact is that the ideal of a mutually devoted relationship between a stepmother and her stepchildren is seldom achieved. The images that we aspire to achieve for ourselves have little bearing on the reality of our family situations.

Stepmothers and stepchildren have a relationship a lot like partners in an arranged marriage. Neither party has much to say about who is on the other end. "The relationships that were part of my life until I married my stepson's father had always been what I called yes-or-no relationships. You got to know the person, and if you liked him, you said yes. You had a relationship. If you didn't, you said no. My husband's older boy was a no. I didn't know what to do. I couldn't get rid of him. I had to deal with him," stated an eight-year stepmother who continues to feel that she and her stepson are not the same kind of people.

"Our chief problem was that we couldn't escape each other. I'm sure we both wondered how we could have any kind of family relationship at all if we were so totally different," she said. He was the first "no" person she was obliged to accept in her private life. "I can say we feel good about each other now. I guess over the years we've gotten used to each other, but I'm not comfortable saying I love him," she added with evident regret. She concluded, after taking a thoughtful pause and drawing a deep breath, "If you had told me when I married my husband that I'd be saying this eight years later, I would have fallen apart. I thought if you didn't love your stepchildren and they didn't love you, it was unacceptable. I was wrong. What my stepson and I have is normal and reasonable. I like him and I respect him and I think he feels the same way about me. But in the beginning I expected much more than that. Now I can see that my expectations were ridiculous."

Breaking away from romantic stereotypes is a monumental accomplishment, yet failing to do so can be crippling, even tragic. A former stepmother whose marriage to a man with three children failed in less than a year now looks back: "My husband and I had no imagination about how to do it. I got right in there and played their mother—cooked meals and gave marching orders. My husband expected me to do that, and so did I. The kids hated it, and eventually, I did, too. Pretty soon I blamed my husband. It wasn't really our fault. We just didn't know what else to do. If we'd looked around for help, it might have worked out differently, but we expected to be a happy family overnight. We refused to give up that dream. It was all or nothing."

Most stepmothers talk about their isolation. Though they may be close to their husbands in every other respect, they hesitate to confide their qualms about stepmothering at the start of a marriage. Other confidants can prove equally unsatisfactory and are often less likely to be sympathetic. "My mother said, 'Well, what did you expect?'" stated a stepmother who found her former best pal no longer a sympathetic listener. It was the old you-made-your-bed-now-lie-in-it reaction that people, maybe mothers in particular, employ when they don't know what else to advise.

Friends without similar family situations can also be disappointing confidants. They often regard the complexities of extended family situations as signs of marriage failure. A stepmother can quickly find that too much tea and sympathy hurts her pride and makes her less likely to bring up the subject again.

Stepmothers aren't always their own best friends either. There are times when most of us feel overwhelmed by our own frustrations. We feel guilty for not loving our stepchildren, flawed by our failure to be selfless, angry with the marriage and the men who brought these problems our way, and powerless. We needn't feel all these emotions at once; any combination can make us feel wretched. Worse, fear of failing our husbands and ourselves leads us to internalize our anguish until it gathers the force of an explosion. Inevitably, most of us let loose. "I have always been a reasonable and controlled person, but when it comes to issues about my husband's daughter, I didn't know I could be so out of hand. I cursed, I hated, I accused, and then I hated myself for the whole spectacle. I looked foolish, and I felt desperate. I'd tried my damnedest and I'd lost," wailed a stepmother who finally blew her cool. She's not alone. This kind of despair or explosion is very common, and it can also be cathartic, marking the end of a phase of confusion and surprise. From then on, a stepmother at least knows what reality she's dealing with.

There are, of course, some stepmothers who do not experience turmoil or stress. They are scarce, however, and I honestly can't say that I've found their approach admirable or easy to relate to. Their stepparenting relationships seemed unrealistically pat and one-dimensional. One such woman said she disliked children, so stepmothering let her in on the fun end of parenting, which for her was buying Madame Alexander dolls and taking her nine-year-old stepdaughter to the circus. She expected the girl to arrive and exit punctually and to demonstrate perfect manners. I got the impression of Shirley Temple making an entrance with a few bars of "On the Good Ship Lollipop" followed by a curtsy. A canopy bed chock-full of dolls was this stepmother's proud contribution to stepmothering. She also said that she had no difficulty with her husband's ex-wife, who quite obviously saw no maternal rival anywhere in sight. She certainly had a positive outlook and a positive experience. Her low expectations were easy to meet. But the majority of stepmothers aren't like her. Fortunately, if they're adaptive, realistic, and patient, they are likely to get more satisfaction out of their stepfamilies as well.

There are simply no quick fixes. Professionals unanimously agree on two invaluable attributes for a stepmother: patience and maturity. Family relations take time. It helps to think of stepmothering as a process rather than as a stance. Relationships change with time and with effort. Suffering in silence or hoping for the best won't help. Since clear roles cannot be assigned to a stepmother or her stepchild, those that result must be genuinely achieved and earned: custom-made, so to speak.

Even professionals sometimes express dismay at the complexity and emotional demands of stepmothering. "I don't know how stepmothers make it," one psychologist said. Psychologists have coined a word for new extended families: "chaos." The term is apt. The marriage of a father, a former head of household, shifts everyone's position in the same way that management changes realign power and loyalties within a corporation. Ripples of anxiety, discontent, subterfuge, and mutiny break out until the new system takes hold. As the stepmother, the newcomer at the top, you feel more denigrated than the others by such chaos. Disoriented by it, you may panic, underestimate your chances for success, and become defensive. However, defensiveness is not your best defense. Patience, perspective, and understanding the emotional currents at work within your stepchildren, your husband, *and yourself* are.

To accept and to become part of a family situation that is unlike the ideal takes extra effort, self-knowledge, and courage. There is more to it than just adapting to a few children. A woman's conditioning about family, sexual roles, and life goals is challenged. Family trailblazing is probably not what you had in mind when you married, but it's as likely to be part of stepmothering as setting an extra place at the table.

The best advantage you can have is a model for stepmothering that is based on reality rather than myth. No woman is adequately prepared to be a stepmother. The idealized versions of stepfamily life don't ring true in practice, and realizing that fact can bring you up short. Also, you've probably never examined the range of emotional and real demands that a stepfamily makes. Most of us enter into stepmothering without theories on how to cope with stepfamily guilt, vacation planning, discipline, visitation schedules, holiday strains, ex-wife relations, and money matters, to mention just a few of the most common areas of concern. We don't consider those things in advance—or even associate them with stepmothering. That's where creating a new, realistic, and flexible model comes into play. It is your best defense against the lows and disappointments that plague us when our steprelations turn out different from some ideal. Different doesn't mean less.

Stepmothering with the proper perspective and expectations can be uplifting, even liberating, from the stereotypes of real mothering and imagined stepmothering that plague us. Learning the differences is where we start.

2

Expectations

Stepmothers-to-be usually have one of three popular preconceptions about stepmothering: (1) Our stepchildren won't really be part of our marriage and lives; (2) our relationship with our stepchildren will be close and familial—like one big happy family; (3) we will love our stepchildren as though they were our own children. With a little experience we realize that all three beliefs are unrealistic.

Others with a familiar ring for you may include: "I thought my husband's daughter and I would be like sisters" or "We agreed not to have any children, so I expected my husband's child would be like my own." The problem with most of these notions is that they don't take into account either that a stepmother sleeps with the child's father or that stepchildren can seldom, if ever, be an emotional substitute for biological children.

THE CHILDREN WON'T BE PART OF MY LIFE

Owning up to the fact that you have married not just a man but his children as well strikes some women as unromantic and not at all the way a marriage should begin. Yet to deny this basic principle about stepchildren is a common evil—and self-deception that can have dire consequences.

"I didn't see the children as being part of our life. I thought they would visit us often and that we'd remember them at Christmas and on their birthdays, but I didn't see them as a factor in our life together," one stepmother recalled. Hers is a common mistake borne out of ignorance and lack of experience. Out of that ignorance comes some of the earliest anguish, even bitterness. "How were we going to be romantic newlyweds, beginning our life together with his children on the scene? Here I had managed my life to avoid settling down and having children so that I could be free of those responsibilities, travel, have a good time, enjoy life. Then I met and married this marvelous man to love and share it all with. But his children seemed to threaten everything I wanted. I felt defeated, gypped," she said.

Stepmothers react this way not because they are cruel or because they dislike children, but because they cannot anticipate the immediate demands of stepmothering. "I think when I got married I thought my husband's daughter, Maria, would be part of my husband's life, but not mine. Frankly, I didn't think about it much," stated a stepmother who was surprised to find her stepchild on the scene and a factor in her life.

When she and her husband dated, he spent time alone with Maria and time alone with her. "I guess I thought it would continue like that. When she suddenly showed up and interfered with my schedule and weekend plans, I didn't like it," she said. Her reaction was to deny the girl's presence and to cling to her old version of how new married life—without children—should be.

So long as she pretended that Maria wasn't partly her responsibility, she felt miserable and alienated. I was mad at every little thing. I harbored a grudge against her and my husband. Her very presence seemed to horn in on my life and pleasure. I constantly wondered, 'What is this child doing here?' "

The strain and tension lessened only when the stepmother made the conscious decision to accept having a stepdaughter. "I couldn't ignore her any longer. I was letting my negative feelings about having her around detract from my marriage and life," she noted. So she switched from the defensive to the offensive. "I stopped being the victim of our relationship; I joined in making plans for her. I didn't treat her like the enemy; instead I tried to manage her presence in my life to my advantage. If she came for the day, I got a sitter and planned dinner out for me and my husband, just little things like that. I asked about her visits ahead of time instead of just waiting to have her arrive and ruin my agenda." It's a familiar story.

"No matter what you think at the beginning," observed a stepmother of eight years, "your stepchildren are an integral part of your life. I wish that someone had told me that. I would have changed my thinking so much sooner. I discovered it by walking into a tornado."

WE'LL BE ONE BIG HAPPY FAMILY

Some stepmothers go overboard in the opposite direction. They gracefully resign themselves to the reality of stepchildren. Magnanimously, they believe that there is enough love and caring to go around. Visions of a cheery household bustling with activity supersede their ideal of a romantic couple. The sound of this idealization can have the same effect on experienced stepmothers as the grating of fingernails scratching across a blackboard.

The problem with the big-happy-family scenario is that it assumes you will love your stepchildren and they will love you in the same way that children and natural mothers usually share affection. The pretty picture that most of us have in mind doesn't take into account stepfamily differences and realities. "My husband, Bob, and I thought that once we all lived together, the kids and I would love each other as much as he and I do, that they'd be sucked into our happiness," a stepmother said. Within two months of her wedding she discovered, "We couldn't have been more wrong. My reactions to the kids were very different from what I'd planned. I liked them well enough, but I didn't love them anywhere near as much as I loved their father. I couldn't overlook their faults, and their daily life and habits got on my nerves much more easily." Furthermore, this stepmother found that they didn't love her like a new mother either. "We got along fine, but the minute Bob or I suggested that we had become a wonderful new family, the kids pulled back. Just using the word 'family' bothered them," she said.

The peculiar reality of stepfamily life became evident to her after she and her husband introduced themselves as a family to their new neighbors. "Why do we say we're a family when we're not?" asked her thirteen-year-old stepdaughter, obviously upset. "We're Dad's kids, and you're Dad's wife, but you're not our mother."

Their stepmother was hurt by what sounded like a rejection of her, but after thinking it over, she decided, "Being a stepmother should be enough. It signifies an honest and real relationship. We don't have to pretend it's more."

She and her husband also settled their image problem to the satisfaction of his children. They still introduce themselves as a family. Her husband explained to the children that new or brief acquaintances don't usually want or need to know your entire family history or marital background. "We project ourselves as a unit, a family, yes," said the stepmother, "but we told the kids that we weren't trying to be something we're not. Bob and I stopped all the big-happy-family references around the house. In private we all know where we're coming from. Our goal is to be real and relaxed."

The best advice is to forget about being one big, happy family. You can create some nice, warm, loving substitute for it, but forget *The Brady Bunch*. Those characters don't live in today's homes or marriages. A lot of fine men, women, children, and modern values do thrive, but their realities are light-years ahead of the images projected by those idealized families. Those stereotypes were hard enough for traditional families to live up to. They are poison for stepfamilies.

THEY'LL BE JUST LIKE MY OWN CHILDREN

Another frequent expectation of stepmothers is to feel that their stepchildren are just like their own. If you don't have biological children, you may be more likely to hope that your stepchildren will substitute for them. Both hopes exceed the bounds of most steprelationships.

The real danger of such expectations is that they typically overshadow the honest relationships that can spring up between a stepmother and her stepchild. Too often we focus on what that relationship isn't instead of what it is. The likely friendships and affection pale in comparison to impossible expectations for a mother-and-child bond. The contrast is unfair. It is a very fine thing to be a good friend to your stepchild, but if you expect to love and be loved like a mother, you may find friendship an unsatisfactory substitute.

One stepmother has a touching recollection about discovering the perimeters of a stepmother's territory. She and her twelve-year-old stepdaughter often cooked together when the girl visited. During these cozy sessions in the kitchen, the stepmother lavished affection and many stories of her own childhood onto her stepdaughter. Then one day the girl asked, "Do you wish you had a little girl?" Her stepmother answered, "I have one. I love you like my own child." The moment passed. During her next visit, her stepdaughter told her, "I told Mom what you said, and she said a stepmother couldn't love someone as much as a real mother." The stepmother wrung her hands and swore that she did love her stepdaughter as much. Later she cried. She said, "Whenever you think your stepchildren are like your own, they bring you up short. It's as though they need to remind you that they have a mother." Even if children love you, they have a mother.

It's unwise for a stepmother to expect or to pretend that her stepchildren will be like her own children, no matter how close the relationship between them might be. They are not her own. They never will be. Thinking otherwise can cause anguish.

No one really understands the special relationship between parents and their biological children. Said counselor Lillian Messinger of the Clarke Institute of Family Relations in Toronto, Canada, childless herself, "I'll never quite understand the parental feelings people have. No matter how much you care for somebody else's kids, it's not the same." Parents can forgive, and children forget, or at least get beyond disappointments and antagonisms with a parent in ways that are less likely with some-one else.

One stepmother was deeply hurt when the stepdaughter she had looked after and cared for, even after she and the girl's father were divorced (and even to the point of helping the girl through the trauma of an abortion), was not invited to her stepdaughter's wedding. "Yet she asked her father, whom she had not seen in years, to escort her down the aisle. The cruelty of it astonished me," stated her stepmother. Cruel, perhaps. Unprecedented, no. A stepmother's ties and duties to her stepchildren are not based on the same basic drives that bind a child and motivate a parent. She must content herself with touching her stepchild's life in different ways and places—and protect herself with appropriate expectations. It takes skill and effort.

I'LL BE A SUPERSTEPMOM

Not all of our expectations have to do with affection or even involvement with our stepchildren. Some are for ourselves, and those, too, can be extraordinarily unrealistic. Women frequently approach stepmothering as a challenge, a test of love they hope to pass for their husband's sake. They put their own interests behind their husband's and stepchildren's. Love, they hope, will conquer all. If taking two toddlers on a honeymoon will prove undying commitment toward a man and his children, so be it, reason some new stepmothers.

It's not surprising that many of us feel keenly disappointed when new relationships with our stepchildren don't live up to our expectations. "I can almost put the words in their mouths," states Thomas Seibt, a family counselor at the California Family Study Center in Burbank. He finds that a never-before-married woman who marries a man with children has the toughest time adjusting to the demands of stepmothering. "She has extremely high expectations and is totally unprepared for what hits her," he contends. Even her self-expectations exceed what's likely or possible. She finds it harder to shrug off disappointment than she imagined it would be. Before marriage she saw a rough patch to cross, but not the whole Grand Canyon. She begins to question whether she's up to the task and the marriage. The disillusionment is alarming.

The children themselves are only part of it. Said a woman who married a man with two toddlers: "I figured when we married that I was equal to the challenge of dealing with the children. In fact, I didn't think it was going to be a big deal at all." In her case, the children weren't a big deal, but visitation schedules, relations with the ex-wife, finances, and marital stress were. Yet the specter of her failure to cope coolly and competently with them humiliated and horrified her.

"The tensions were unbelievable. It was a nightmare. I just threw up my hands and said, 'Okay, I was wrong about myself. I'm not up to it. I can't take it. I know I can't expect my husband to give up his children, so we'll have to get a divorce.' I felt the end of the marriage would be my punishment for my inability to cope." Two years later, she is glad she stuck things out, but she admitted, "I wouldn't have made it if I hadn't seriously changed my expectations."

False expectations of one kind or another are the root of most stepmothers' discontent. Emily and John Visher, a husband-and-wife counseling team, both stepparents, have coauthored a leading guidebook for therapists who work with stepfamilies. In *Stepfamilies: A Guide to Working with Stepparents and Stepchildren* they point out that stepmothers usually hope for too much. Stepmothers, they maintain, expect to make up to the children for their suffering during their parents' divorce, and they want to create a new, close-knit family that will compensate for the one that is gone. In short, they try to make everybody happy, which is a well-known prescription for emotional disaster.

The Vishers consider these goals to be "so unrealistic that they cause difficulties which jeopardize the life of a stepfamily."

It helps to understand a "superstepmom's" motives, which are powerful. A stepmother climbs far out on a limb in order to prove she isn't wicked. Every woman interviewed for this book mentioned, without prompting, her dread of being considered a wicked stepmother. Mean myths about stepmothers are securely embedded in our consciousness, thanks to Cinderella and that gang of childhood characters we grew up with. She who comes between mother and child—if only on weekends—feels obliged to be perfect. In fact, most stepmothers will verge on the masochistic in order to assure themselves and anyone who's watching that they are *not wicked*.

Annie, a stepmother of three youngsters who live with their mother, kept the baby she had with her husband sleeping in a crib in their bedroom for nearly two years, while two empty bedrooms across the hall, reserved for her visiting stepchildren on weekends, were empty. "I didn't want my stepchildren to think that our son was supplanting them or invading their space," she explained. Had the children been hers, they would have had to accommodate the new baby, but because they were her stepchildren, Annie felt awkward. More than merely conscientious, she went ridiculously far to prove that she was neither mean nor wicked.

Scaling down our expectations to a realistic level takes understanding and a willingness to accept less than the cozy family ideal that has fostered our fantasies. It's not easy. First, you must identify your high hopes and be able to abandon those that are unlikely to be achieved.

Facing these changes and revamping our basic expectations almost overnight is a daunting proposition. If it's any solace, your fellow family members—your husband and his children—have probably beaten you to it. At the time of divorce or death they had to reckon with changes and ruined expectations. But because a stepmother's timing and vantage point are different from theirs, she may feel alone and frightened by the adjustment she must make.

You don't have to accept a grim or negative outlook, if that's their idea of reality, but you must be realistic. Once you trim your expectations down to realistic proportions, stepmothering is a much less disappointing proposition. You may even discover relationships and rewards that you didn't expect.

3

Guilt

uilt often is the stepmother's primary emotion. It comes from many sources. The inability to achieve your expectations about your new family makes you feel flawed, unworthy—and guilty. If you don't feel affection for your stepchildren, that makes you feel guilty. Sometimes you may find yourself wishing that they weren't around, and that makes you feel guilty, too. If you and your husband quarrel over how to handle them or when to see them, you feel more guilty. It adds up.

If you were involved with your husband before or during his divorce, you invariably feel guilty. Though you may feel blameless about his divorce and confident about the rightness of your marriage (you remind yourself that no "other woman" breaks up a really good marriage), you see the children, innocent of the foibles of their parents, suffer just the same. Just being witness to so much devastation can make you feel like a home wrecker.

Furthermore, your stepchildren may regard you as such, which doesn't help either. A disreputable image can have a crippling effect on your effectiveness and self-esteem in the family. If you met your husband after his marriage ended, you feel guilty just the same for requiring that your stepchildren adjust yet again to adult fortunes. Even second wives of widowed men feel guilty. Intervening anywhere in a mother-and-child relationship, even in the memory of a beloved dead mother, causes guilt.

One woman told of how she took personally her stepson's difficulty in adjusting to college life. "I always regarded him as a troubled boy on account of his parents' divorce and his father's marriage to me. I blamed myself. If I was happy with life and we visited Drake [her stepson] and he seemed low, I felt enormously guilty." However, after Drake was out on his own, this stepmother began to see that much of her guilt was unnecessary. Drake had personality problems well outside his relations with her and his father. "He was an unsociable boy with low self-esteem by most standards for boys his age. I felt sorry for him. I still do, and my husband and I try to help, but I don't blame myself anymore," she stated. When the boy's grandparents told her that Drake had not been a cheerful or outgoing child even while his parents' marriage was intact, it came as a great relief. "It wasn't my fault. I felt exonerated," she said.

We often don't have a whole sense of a stepchild's personality, complete with the behavior patterns that might explain that his or her conduct is unrelated to us. But our tendency to assume responsibility for his or her problems or unhappiness only intensifies our guilt.

Stepmothers usually want to get involved quickly with their stepchildren and to be expert about them, able to explain their moods and reactions, to analyze and make sense of their personalities and behavior as they would a jigsaw puzzle. But enthusiasm isn't enough to give you a proper understanding of a child and his or her emotional makeup. It takes time. So there's no use seeing yourself as central to a problem that is not your fault. Accepting the blame probably just inhibits your ability to recognize the real reasons behind your stepchild's reactions and to take steps that can help.

A child who has habitual social problems may need help sorting out those difficulties that legitimately stem from his stepfamily, but a stepmother should never become a scapegoat for them. Many children of divorce and remarriage cope admirably with the experience and continue their lives uncrippled by it. Children need support, help, and understanding, but a stepmother shouldn't become a handy excuse for unhappiness or failure. She doesn't have to accept or adopt it as her cause for guilt.

Guilt often makes stepmothers take a servile approach to their stepchildren, trying to win trust and affection with self-conscious concern and selflessness. The outcome is usually frustrating, because stepmothers aren't likely to receive in proportion to their giving. "It's a thankless job because no matter what you do, nobody is going to thank you for marrying his or her parent," warns Lillian Messinger.

A common guilt is feeling responsible for the distance between a father and his children. "I feel that if I were their mother, I wouldn't care if they were here every weekend. But as things are, I do, and I feel bad about it. They could be first in his life if he wasn't remarried," said a stepmother, ready to assume guilt because her husband is no longer married to his first wife and living with his children.

A stepmother cannot see herself as the *cause* of every deviation from old family models. She is just another player in these new stepfamilies, alongside everyone else. It's a grave mistake to see yourself as the cause of the differences. Personalizing every new situation will also prevent you from discovering the real reasons behind problems and working for solutions.

Some guilts are unreasoning. Those expectations for loving and being loved are the worst. Cynthia, an extremely composed and sophisticated woman, spoke dispassionately of her disappointment with her husband's two grown children: "I've wanted them to feel our home is a place for them, that they aren't imposing on us." To this end she stocks the pantry with their favorite foods before visits, shops painstakingly for their birthday and Christmas presents, and plays hostess to their friends and guests. But Cynthia seldom gets anything in return for her efforts. She has never received a personal gift or direct thanks from either of them. "Because they're my husband's children, I treat them as friends, but it's torture. If other people acted so badly, I would turn them away," she said. Her husband, who disapproves of his children's treatment of his wife and says so, could be forgiven a lapse in his affection toward children who treat his wife so inconsiderately, yet Cynthia crucifies herself over her negative feelings toward them. Her composure cracked when, close to tears, she guiltily confessed what she considers a failure in her character: "I don't love them."

According to a leading stepfamily authority, "It's unrealistic to feel you have to love your stepchildren, even if you do have to care for them. If it ends up that you love them and they love you, then that's a nice bonus. But it can't always be that way. You can have a happy marriage without it. Stepmothers should be loving, respecting people, caring people in these relations, but they don't have to love those kids. The marriage is between you and the father. You promise to love him, not his children."

4

Husbands

A husband determines much of his wife's step-mothering experience. If the children are beastly but he is involved and supportive of her, she will find that stepmothering isn't so bad. It works the other way, too. If the children are angelic but he is an ineffectual ally, she may well find stepmothering a misery.

Unlike natural mothering, stepmothering is exclusively a project for couples. A stepmother has a parental relationship only through her husband, the father. They're his kids, not hers, and she has him to thank—for better or for worse—for their very presence in her life. Initially, he sets the tone of their relationship. His attitudes and actions determine how effective his wife can be, especially in matters of discipline and authority. Granted, a stepmother can botch a few things on her own, but she cannot be successful, even at her very best, without her husband's support.

ROLES

A remarried husband also has a tough role to play. His marriage catapults him into a world of family concerns, negotiations, and diplomacy for which he may be poorly prepared. Your reliance on his help and influence makes his an even more difficult position to be in.

Everything depends on him. He is expected to serve as a confidant and an ally of his wife during trying times for her—hard times that he has at least indirectly caused. After all, *he* ushered his children and former mate into his new wife's life. Yet most husbands are uneasy in their dual role as perpetrator and comforter. Guilt and loyalty pull at them as they move through marital and family crises. The array of delicate and explosive family relations on all sides comes as a shock to them. It's not so much that they are a cloddish lot; it's just that they have no experience in such matters. In former marriages their wives were most likely to tend to the children's emotional affairs. Family issues, such as vacations, were less likely to be divisive when everyone's interests were the same.

Remarried fathers soon find that being in the middle is no fun. Ironically, their difficulty is similar to stepmothers'. Nothing in their experience or upbringing has prepared them to be in this spot. Said the second wife of a man with two teenage children, "My husband was very aware of everyone's different interests, but he couldn't know what it was really going to be like. He wasn't aware *enough*." One Thanksgiving he tried valiantly to shuttle the fifty miles between his ex-wife's home where his children live and his home and new wife in the city. He even ate two dinners. "But his kids didn't think they had enough time with him, I was put out, and he was exhausted. It was a no-win situation for everybody," she stated.

The men in these spots are initially surprised by how much time and effort they must spend orchestrating people and events just to keep the peace. Like stepmothers, they can be overwhelmed by the complexities. They may need help sensing sore points in their wives and children.

A stepmother immediately finds that her husband's attitude toward his children can diminish or elevate her role in the family. Consequently, his parental style and authority have a marked impact on their marriage, usually much to his astonishment. The stepmother is surprised, sometimes traumatized, by how deeply conflicts about parenting can drive a wedge into her relationship with her new husband. Early in marriages, when neither partner is on the lookout for trouble, stepparenting problems have a way of sneaking up on a couple. One new stepmother was understandably distraught when her four-year-old stepdaughter climbed into the newlyweds' getaway car to ride home from their wedding party with her father and his new bride, because the child's mother had not made travel arrangements for her. "I could have killed him, and we'd only been married an hour," said the former bride.

CONFLICT

The way a father handles his children greatly affects how a stepmother will respond to them. It's almost as important as the children's personalities. "My stepdaughter can be a tough kid to love on her own, but my real complaints with her are always about the way my husband deals with her," remarked the custodial stepmother of a ten-year-old. In her opinion, her husband has a neurotic attachment to his daughter. "He identifies so closely with her that if I raise my voice at her for messing up the living room, he jumps in to defend her. She and I could work things out, but the triangle is impossible. I always feel it's him and her versus me."

Such jealousies and conflicts occur among natural parents and children, too, but in natural families they don't have the potential for anguish and destruction that they have in stepfamilies. Beth, the stepmother of an eleven-year-old boy who visits her and his father regularly, said, "I can handle my husband, Robert, and I can handle my stepson, Andrew. I happen to really like Andrew. But put the two of them together, and I can't handle it." Her grievance is common. She believes that her husband overindulges Andrew, even takes advantage of his vulnerabilities.

"Robert won't let him grow up. He even refuses to send him to camp. He wants to keep Andrew dependent, so he'll keep needing his father and be controllable," stated Beth, who pleads guilty to playing amateur psychologist more than she would like. She believes she has a more objective view of Andrew than Robert does, but if she makes critical observations or suggests more freedom for him, Robert rejects her criticism and accuses her of being jealous. "When it comes to Andrew, Robert is crazy," said Beth.

In one extreme instance, Robert announced to their friends, in Andrew's presence, that he and his wife would not accept a job transfer because Andrew worried about dying alone in a plane crash on the way to visit them. "Robert should have told him about the safety of modern air travel and the positive aspects of flying. Instead, he reinforced his phobia about flying, and he was letting Andrew, a kid, determine his professional future and our lives. I was furious." When she tried to discuss the subject, Robert accused her of trying to manipulate him in order to move away from Andrew. Wounded and feeling at a loss, she dropped the subject, but the issue continued to bother her.

Not surprisingly, her negative feelings have invaded her relationship with Andrew. She admitted, "I've become adamant about always being right. If we're out on a drive and Andrew thinks he has seen a mountain goat, I tell him, 'No. It was a deer.'" During a recent Scrabble game, Beth insisted on proving and winning every point in the rulebook. She even disputed Andrew's recollection of the color of the dress she wore on some past occasion.

Afflicted with parental and marital misunderstandings, a stepmother often reels from the pain a husband's distrust can cause. To her, it is a betrayal, one that she sometimes returns in kind by striving thereafter, as accused, to be less caring and sharing with a stepchild. It becomes a vicious circle and a silent war.

To the husband, the separation of his relationship with his child from that with his wife may be understandable. He has already adjusted once to the role of lone parent. If the parental relationship he shared with his child's mother is divided or poisoned, as happens in some divorces, he may not expect his new wife to parent very much. He may even pride himself on being the only person who can keep his child's best interests in mind. A stepmother may feel closed out. It's little solace to know that the problem is her husband's, not her own.

GUILT

Guilt is the common denominator among remarried fathers. It is a natural emotion for divorced parents, but fathers who remarry—the step that signifies the end of the former family—often suffer from guilt to an extreme degree. Its influence can determine a man's approach to his children—and his wife.

A father's guilt makes the barrier between husband and wife over stepmothering issues even less penetrable. Guilt often blinds divorced fathers. Some men are almost debilitated by it. "I see men go to their children on their knees," said a family psychologist, who explains the negative effect a parent's guilty behavior has on the children. "They begin thinking that something wrong has been done to them if their father acts this way. It makes everybody feel worse. Nonetheless, it's a very common reaction." When a parent follows a course of action, such as divorce and remarriage, that disrupts the life of his child, guilt enters in no matter how grim the personal alternatives for the parent might have been. Unable to reconcile their personal satisfaction and fatherly feelings, remarried husbands tend to sacrifice themselves, and often their new wife's interests, in the process of their self-flagellation. Men without custody of their children—the overwhelming majority—suffer the most. Terrified of losing their children entirely, they will go to any length to win and secure affection. Simply put, they set out to be Superdads—indulgent, all fun. Discipline becomes a dirty word—if it exists at all. Men who once barked orders at their kids like drill sergeants suddenly turn to jelly when it's time to ask a child to carry her dirty plate to the sink.

From a stepmother's point of view, Superdads are a dangerously deranged lot. They forget about romance, private time, sometimes even sex. Said one stepmother: "When my husband and I went on vacation without his son, my husband spent every minute saying, 'Wouldn't it be nice if Stevie were here?' My feeling was, no, it wouldn't be so great. I was glad he wasn't with us, but I knew better than to say so. When I did remark that certain trips should be just for us, my husband wouldn't hear of it. He'd start saying how much fun Stevie would have in the water or in the mountains, wherever we were. If I disagreed, I was the meanie. Frankly, I don't think he wants Stevie along with us all the time either, but he needs to hear himself say he does, to prove he's a wonderful father."

Such guilt-inspired excesses typically cause negative or even perverse reactions in a stepmother. It alarms her to see her husband lose control of the elementary order of parent-child relations. He is, after all, her only advocate in an extended family, so his weakness threatens her enormously. "I have had my fill of hearing how wonderful these kids are," remarked the one-year stepmother of two young children. "'According to my husband, Junior walks on water. Obviously, he doesn't, and I wouldn't want him around every minute if he did."

COMPETITION

A stepmother may feel competitive for her husband's attention and affection if he is overprotective or allows his children to dominate his home and married life. Husbands who allow guilt to inspire a stepchild-dominated environment in their homes or during visits create a competitive atmosphere that can be poisonous for stepmother-stepchild relations.

The result is agonizing. "One of the most difficult things that happens to a stepmother is that after she marries a man she finds she takes a backseat while he courts his children. It's cruel. Her courtship ends, and she watches someone else's, and resents it," notes Lillian Messinger.

Tobie was miserable when her husband began taking his children away to a nearby resort every weekend after their wedding. "I stayed home alone in town. He explained that the kids weren't ready for me yet. I can't tell you how furious and how bad I felt," she said. Often neither husband nor wife quite understands what is happening. Tensions and resentment just rush in. Emotions flare quickly because both partners, new to the marriage, are vulnerable. The husband feels tugged from two directions, and a stepmother feels petty to be jealous of the children. Rather than confront each other, they keep their own counsel and commonly argue over something else, such as who takes out the garbage.

"I was miserable over how much attention Dave lavished on his children, but I couldn't bring it up with him. I was ashamed that it bothered me. He was having problems with his ex and the kids, and I didn't want to join his list of problems. But inside I was deeply disappointed in him," stated a stepmother who lacked the courage to tackle problems she could barely define.

Stepmothers frequently say they are made uncomfortable when their husbands hold hands or put their arms around their children, while they, the wives, hover on the side or walk two paces behind. "I always feel like the fifth wheel when we take my twelve-year-old stepdaughter to the movies. My husband holds her hand. They walk out of the theater arm in arm. It's awkward for me, as if I'm on their date," said one stepmother. She was quick to add, "I've never been a jealous person. My husband has lunch with old girlfriends and even drinks occasionally with his ex-wife. Those things don't bother me. But when we're out with his daughter, I feel cross and left out." Idle jealousy is not the root of her problem. Rather, when a stepmother needs assurance, outward signs of solidarity take on a disproportionate significance. Embraces, hand-holding, and other displays of affection between a father and child aren't wrong, nor should they offend a stepmother—unless they exacerbate uncertainties that already exist in the marriage.

Husbands are often casual in assuming their wives understand their relationship to their children. The stepmother without children is clearly at a disadvantage. If she's never been married before, things are even more difficult for her. She does not understand why her new husband is out on the beach watching the sunset with his son when she is inside scrubbing the lobster steamer. Yet her husband probably doesn't know she is hurt and fuming. "Wives who haven't been married before want to have the goodies of a first marriage, the fun and the romance. And why shouldn't they want it? But everybody has to work for it," Messinger states.

Working at these marriages usually means being extremely open about your jealousies and vulnerabilities and sometimes risking a confrontation with your husband in order to work through problems. Though a husband may initially scoff at the outward sign (such as hand-holding) that causes your distress, he should be alerted to your feelings. Telling him will help him to understand your reactions, and he may be able to dispel some of your fears and anxieties with reassurance. He will at least be better able to take your viewpoint into consideration.

If he strongly disagrees with your perceptions, you may need to reexamine the cause of your insecurities. If a gulf exists between his point of view and yours or if you have the nagging idea that your reactions may be rooted in your own psyche, professional guidance can probably help. Of course, a professional may not be able to put every little competitive urge and insecurity to rest, but he can probably encourage you and your husband to establish a closer relationship about stepfamily matters.

PRIORITIES

One stepmother went through hell because she felt that she and her marriage were always second to her stepchildren. After she and her husband liquidated half of their financial assets in order to move into a bigger house to accommodate their visits and scheduled their own vacations to accommodate the children's schedules (they had even taken them on their honeymoon), this stepmother finally sought advice from her minister. He summoned her and her husband and instructed both of them to put their lives and marriage first. "It's not that every choice must be a statement or that we ever put down the children, but the bottom line is that this marriage comes ahead of other things," she said. When her husband searched his soul and adapted to the new family value system, initially to save his marriage, his wife stated, "My life changed almost overnight. I felt we had a life for the first time."

A husband should give his marriage priority for many reasons. Ironically, a sound second marriage does more than benefit husband and wife. It also gives stepchildren a sense of well-being, though this point is often overlooked. As a divorced parent probably knows best, a weak marriage has a negative effect on kids, who have uncannily good antennae for detecting strains and tension. Marital discord puts a damper on the best of family times. Children who have witnessed the disintegration of one marriage are cautious about allying themselves to another couple until they can feel certain that it is stable.

The theory here is good enough. Yet fathers, especially those burdened with guilt, are slow to communicate the strength of their new marriage to their children. Defensively, they avoid making statements of any sort—by word or deed—about their new lives. At first glance, the omission seems a kindness, as though a happy second marriage would somehow betray a child. But children who aren't clear about the status of their father's marriage frequently assume that they have some jurisdiction over matters, or worse, that their stepmother is subject to their approval, an assumption that stepmothers consider degrading and inappropriate.

A father who gives his child veto power over his choice of mate does everyone a disservice. He undermines the authority of both adults, not to mention his own happiness, should his child rule against his choice. In addition, he wrongs the child by allowing him or her to take responsibility for adult relations. He falsely inflates the child's sense of power in the world. Ultimately, improper privileges are upsetting to children of divorce, who have already lost the order of a nuclear home and should be spared the loss of parental authority as well.

I am not suggesting the tactless flaunting of a happy marriage at a child who is left behind in a troubled home, or the disparaging of the marriage that produced him; but the point needs to be made that parent-child relations are absolute and constant on their own terms. Consequently, the marriage is equally independent of a child's intervention or approval. It works both ways. Putting children in their proper position, in these cases at the receiving end of parental concern and affection, is both instructive and reassuring. Unfortunately, these principles usually don't become obvious to remarried husbands until all hell breaks loose, which is typically what happens when family loyalties are unclear. Invariably, even the most well intentioned partners learn the hard way.

Indignities mounted up one after another for Alexandra, the stepmother of three children in their early twenties, before she and her husband agreed to take action. Her two stepdaughters rifled through her clothing and personal belongings and slept in her bed when she was out of town. Eventually she put locks on the closet and bedroom doors. "I ranted and raved," Alexandra said, "but my husband thought we were just a bunch of bickering women. He didn't want to see that his girls could be so ugly."

Eventually he had no choice. One afternoon both girls cornered Alexandra, a petite woman, in the kitchen. "It was a locker-room scene," she stated. "They shoved me around, taunting me, saying that I'd married their father for his money. Things like that." When her husband came home that night, Alexandra gave him an ultimatum. "I told him it was them or me." Her husband, who agreed that his daughters' behavior was out of line, told them that they would have to move out of the house. He and Alexandra were finally clear about one thing: their marriage came first.

Granted, Alexandra's stepdaughters were old enough to be expected to make accommodations outside their father's home, but just the same, it was a bitter pill for her husband. "He and I had waited four years to marry so that those girls would be grown up enough to accept his remarriage. He had bent over backward to make their lives easier and look what they did to him," she noted sadly.

It's important to note that even in Alexandra's situation, where a father took a strong position against his daughters, they were not lost to him. Though one girl stayed out of touch for six months, she finally came around to visit her father and Alexandra, and she has resumed a more normal relationship with them since. Despite her father's worst fears, she did not permanently reject him. The natural order of parent-child relations, even in extended families, invariably triumphs.

YOUR PART

Stepmothers frequently need to reduce their expectations of their husband's control over their children. Like most non-parents, they may have unrealistic notions of the demands a parent can reasonably make of a child. Divorced fathers, especially those without custody of their children, have a distinct disadvantage if their authority is undermined in the children's home. Obviously, no matter how much a husband loves a woman, he can't exact the same affection toward her from his children. But affection aside, the best of husbands, and not bad fathers either, often cannot solicit courtesy, good manners, or good behavior from their children toward their wives. A husband simply isn't God, even with his children. Even if it's reasonable to expect a stepchild to look you, the stepmother, in the eye, say hello, or drop you a thank-you note, he cannot always make it happen. The wife who ascribes such automatic powers to her husband or confuses them with his affection and respect for her will be frustrated over and over again.

You can look to your husband for support of your married relationship and a growing understanding and recognition of your role as stepmother. "When I married Annie, I thought of her as becoming my wife. My kids were my kids. 'Stepmother' was just some dumb title for her," observed a husband who has changed his point of view in three years. "After watching her and knowing the problems with my kids that we've worked out together, the word now has some meaning for me." Husbands aren't necessarily to blame for misrepresenting the position. They just didn't realize what the role requires either. The best you can offer each other is sympathy and understanding while you learn together. You're both in the same boat.

COMMUNICATION

Marriage partners in stepfamilies need to discuss their points of view and to become aware of each other's positions. However, good intentions often inhibit the kind of open conversation couples need most. New marriage partners, full of enthusiasm and goodwill, mistakenly try to contain and conceal their anxieties. Good sportsmanship works against them if it obscures their willingness to recognize complex problems and work together toward solutions. There's little room in these situations for coyness and laissez-faire attitudes.

It's also a fact that men are usually not so attuned to emotional currents and issues as women are. Frequently, they need a little prodding. "My husband didn't think in psychological terms very much" is how the custodial stepmother of a fifteen-year-old girl remembers it. "He just took things day by day without examining them. But when I moved in with him and his daughter, it was like a crash course in family psychology. There were tears from both of us every day. He couldn't believe it. I know he thought he'd made a mistake, and his first reaction was not to get involved. But I talked and I talked and I talked to make him see what was happening and that he would have to help. He has gotten much better at it."

Fortunately, most men do. Stan, who caused his wife, Tobie, so much pain by taking his children to the seaside every weekend without her, now looks back uncomfortably on those troubled times. "I was wrong a lot. I refused to try counseling, but now I can see I was wrong. It would have helped us a lot. I just didn't know what to expect. I had never thought about it all before."

A smart mate will realize that it's usually necessary to coax her husband into these waters. He may not volunteer. Don't play games or manipulate; just brief and advise your husband about stepparenting problems as you see them. Think of yourselves as joint chiefs. And remember that in critical situations, dominated by high emotions and heated disagreements, professional advice can help.

Take comfort from the fact that remarried husbands are usually more willing to listen and to work at relationships and solutions to family problems than men who have never been married before. Your husband's past experience and divorce are likely to have increased his awareness of the need for working together at marriage. He's also likely to take marriage and family concerns very seriously. Women married to divorced fathers may find in the end that their husband's commitment, patience, and determination match and eventually help to overcome the frustrations of stepfamily life. "They're in these marriages for much better reasons than they had for the first ones, and they want them to work," states Thomas Seibt of the California Family Study Center in Burbank.

In short, couples who learn to deal jointly with stepfamily problems shore up their own relationship. Such partners gain a whole new understanding about the way families work, and to some extent they become more enlightened about themselves. Though almost everyone agrees that the emotions and anxieties that can force a stepfamily couple to self-examination are hellish, the way out of those agonies can be an uplifting and expanding experience for a marriage. A husband cannot always change his children, but he can reinforce his marriage to withstand the strains they put on it. That is something no stepmother can do alone.

5

The Wicked Ex-Wife

A husband's ex-wife is the woman most step-mothers love to hate. They relish the chance to have a go at her, and in some cases, she deserves it. Saying so is bound to get some backs up, but it's only fair that stepmothers finally have their say.

To hear stepmothers tell it, "She's (neurotic, batty, wacko, a real psychotic, absolutely nuts)." Pick one of the above. These descriptions char-acterize a large percentage of ex-wives floating around if you can believe what stepmothers tell you. While some of these exes may be certifi-able lunatics, or in shaky emotional straits, it seems unlikely that they are *all* nuts.

Though it can be satisfying, there's no trick to badmouthing your husband's former wife. Stepmothers have an arsenal of personal dirt about her, provided by their husbands at a time when the worst things are better remembered than the best. God forbid that anyone with bad intentions should be privy to as much personal information about us—or anybody. It's not easy, and a few lapses are excusable, even therapeutic, but a stepmother is better off taking the high road when it comes to matters pertaining to her husband's ex-wife. (We might as well say "their" or "her" ex, since it seems as though you've both been married to her.)

If you can't resist taking a crack at her from time to time, go ahead, but know your company when you do so and don't expect anyone except another stepmother to enjoy it as much as you do. I know a couple who privately call their ex "Lovely," because her behavior isn't. It does them a world of good and it doesn't hurt anybody in a relationship where a little fun and irreverence are well earned.

Still, there is a serious side to having an ex-wife in your life. "A second marriage is always tied to the first, and the ex-wife relationship, especially where children are concerned, keeps the first marriage alive in the second," explains Lillian Messinger. To a stepmother, the earlier wife is a little totem of the past, a reminder of a life and love that went before. While the husband who knew her has few romantic notions left about his ex-wife, his new wife may create her own mythology about her: why he married her, why they split, why she doesn't braid her daughter's hair. Don't think too much; it simply doesn't pay.

But, of course, you can't forget about her. She does exist, and that's the problem. Stepchildren are a constant reminder of her.

They usually mention their mother the way they'd trot out a prize collie for your inspection: to see how you react.

Even if the children don't mention their mother (which seems awfully artificial, if tactful), they're likely to escort her into your life in other invisible ways, like a communicable disease. Kids have an uncanny knack for this. They like to see you squirm a little, to spark a little drama. One stepdaughter reminded her stepmother every time she was within ten miles of the town where her parents were married of the significance of that location. Sure, it bugged her a little at first. Her weekend would have been complete without her narration of the geography. But once she got better at reacting to the reference, it went away.

It's surprising how many stepchildren know where they were conceived and how many make sure to tell their stepmother. Needless to say, it goes over like a lead balloon if they remind you, as one teenage stepson did when his dad and stepmother were headed for a vacation to the same spot, but it shouldn't be a big deal. Children are entitled to have a sense of their own history; nobody can take *that* away from them. The best strategy with stepchildren who indulge incessantly in such references is to ignore them or discuss the habit with them directly. Get off the defense and onto the offense.

Psychologists agree that there's not enough scientific research about the effect of ex-wives on stepmothers to allow many broad pronouncements about these relationships to be made, but they do advise second wives to avoid getting caught up in comparisons and rivalries. Ruth Neubauer, Ed.D., president of the New York Association for Marriage and Family Therapy, strongly suggests that second wives steer clear of competing with their exes. They should also, she adds, resist the temptation to style themselves to be better rematches. "Your real self will come through, so trying to be something you're not—or the first wife wasn't—isn't going to work," she maintains. It just pulls the knot of stepmother anxiety tighter.

Lillian Messinger states, "I don't think a woman can be in a second marriage without her husband sharing his history with her, but if she becomes obsessed about it, worrying about things like how big his ex-wife's breasts were, how she performed in bed, all the intimate details, it can become pathological. It isn't productive." Revisionist history can be just as deadly. Don't expect your husband to say that everything was terrible. There must have been some good times. If it had all been bad, there would probably be something wrong with him now, too.

A lot about being a stepmother has to do with being a second wife. Stepmothers feel powerless to affect matters that the ex typically controls, such as visitation, alimony, the upkeep of the children, and a slew of other often annoying arrangements and logistics that touch their lives regularly. An ex-wife's attempts to indoctrinate her children against their stepmother is also quite common. No woman can be expected to welcome this intrusion into her life. It is frequently hidden or impossible to anticipate at the start of a marriage. Divorced men typically appear to have lives of their own, but remarriage seems to activate their ex-wives and can release a penchant for bitchiness.

Carlin met her husband, Bob, after his divorce from his wife, Linda, who had left him. Their two children, nine and three, lived with Linda and her new husband eighty miles away. Bob religiously followed a visitation agreement that was part of his and Linda's divorce agreement. It specified that he could see the children every Tuesday, one weekend a month, plus one additional weekend day. Linda refused to adjust the schedule by combining consecutive days to substitute for a weekend or to bridge a weekend and the upcoming Tuesday, so Bob and Carlin drove eighty miles roundtrip to pick up and return his children ten times every month.

"It was ludicrous," Carlin said. "I think Bob was so traumatized at the time of the divorce that he was just thankful he was going to get to see the kids at all. Now he sees things more clearly, but at the time he wasn't going to buck any agreement that gave him the right to see them regularly, so he was stuck with it. I didn't want him not to see the kids, but I sure wanted him to say, 'Wait a minute, lady—you're being ridiculous.' I got on with the kids, but I was so furious with Linda and her terms that I was a wreck whenever we picked them up."

When she and Bob got married on a Thursday, Linda insisted that the kids visit their father on the following weekend, as planned, or that he forfeit his monthly right to spend a weekend with them. That's when Carlin began to take things personally. "It was nothing but just mean and perverse," Carlin asserted. Visitation was Linda's big stick—and she used it. Everything was nonnegotiable. Linda called all the shots. "It's the powerlessness that gets you," stated Carlin.

It's fair to ask if her husband couldn't have intervened somewhere along the line here, but that, as we've discussed, is another story. The fact is, he didn't, and Carlin resented it. Her negative feelings followed a well-worn emotional path back to the kids, on whom, in her heart, she wearily laid the blame for so much aggravation. "I felt they were the ex-wife's children, far more than my husband's. They even look like her," she said, reacting emotionally instead of rationally.

Though such a reaction is human and not wholly illogical, there is real danger in it. Negative feelings about a child's mother shouldn't be allowed to determine your response to your stepchildren. Like other prejudices, they harm you as well as them. They prevent you from treating your stepchildren as individuals, an especially unfair burden on young stepchildren, who do not consciously mirror their mother's attitudes, as adolescents might. Perhaps worse, they inhibit you from reacting freely, a vital requirement for good stepparenting. When a stepmother locks herself into a sour and defensive position, even if the causes are well understood, everyone is cheated, she as much as the others. This may be how mean stepmothers get their start.

I interviewed one stepmother who had good reason to despise her husband's ex-wife. The natural mother had abandoned her children to her husband, then snatched them away after the stepmother had made a home for them. The ex destroyed property, stole money, spread lies, started court actions, took drugs, threw the kids out again, bore an illegitimate child, and abused the stepmother on the phone. The list was endless. I saw some of the letters and legal documents, enough to convince me that the ex hadn't driven the second wife to wild imaginings about her. Amazingly, the stepmother was still a sane, convincing woman. She was bitter at her husband's ex-wife, as she had a right to be.

The tragedy was that the stepmother seemed no longer able to distinguish her stepchildren from their mother. She hated them all. Things are never clear-cut in these situations. Obviously, the natural mother's problems had taken their toll on the children, who showed a few wounds for spending eleven years in such a snakepit. But they were victims, too. The stepmother couldn't prevent the harm done. The ex-wife's conduct had so obviously determined this stepmother's attitudes and reflexes that she could describe her stepdaughter only as "just like her mother. I can't stand her." Yet this had also been the little girl she recalled was once "affectionate and needy. She clung to me, and she was very sweet. I bought her a pony and taught her to ride." As we've already discussed, stepmothers don't have to love their stepchildren. But I'm not convinced this girl's positive or negative qualities were given the chance to emerge.

Ex-wives often can and do create a combat atmosphere. Their antics and attacks—legal, public, or mercilessly waged through the children—often have an ironically positive effect on a second marriage. Though it may damage the quality of civilized life, the battle-zone mentality—everybody to battle stations, the ex is at it again—can serve to unite a husband and wife. If an ex-wife's intention is to damage, she ought to think again. Drama heightens romance. "We quickly felt our home was a fortress. It was him and me against the world," said one second wife of the days when challenging legal correspondence and spiteful phone calls from their ex was a common occurrence. "It was miserable, but we were committed to persevering and weathering this woman's attacks. We had a sense of mission." No woman would recommend turmoil with an ex-wife as tonic for a marriage, but there are worse things for it and some interesting side effects. An ex tends to erode what guilt and goodwill a husband may have felt toward her. All a stepmother has to do is sit back and watch.

MOTIVES

Ex-wives obviously have their side of these stories, too. Divorce is followed by a difficult personal period for everyone. Though a stepmother is entitled to her opinions and philosophy on parenting, the children belong to their natural mother. The way she raises them is plainly her prerogative. Perhaps stepmothers without their own children expect more of natural mothers than is reasonable, too. Women who have never kept house for a family or bustled two toddlers out in the morning may set unrealistically high standards for mothers who actually do. Ex-wives should get the benefit of the doubt.

Yet divorced mothers frequently do, it seems, abdicate certain aspects of mothering when a family breaks up. Their world is often shattered, and they seem to relegate their children to the back burner. Their husband's remarriage doesn't whet their appetite for parenting either. One stepmother, who had always heard the ex extolled as an especially good cook, was surprised to learn from her visiting stepchildren that now they made most of their own meals and ate them on the floor in front of the television. Stepmothers frequently complain about how badly the children are dressed. Complaints about table manners run a close second.

"Her reward is not the same when the family's not all there," explains Messinger, who advises stepmothers to take it easy on ex-wives in this area. "What right do you have to judge what kind of mother your husband's ex-wife is?"

The general desire to disparage accounts for some stepmothers' readiness to heap reproach on their husband's ex-wife, but a stepmother's concern usually goes beyond that. She romantically sees her stepchildren as an extension of her husband, and if she has adopted them as family members of some sort, then she has the right to care about them—without apologies—even if her criticism and input run up against the mother's performance. Her biggest challenge is to influence the children in constructive ways without fanning fires with the ex-wife or becoming obsessed. Know your limits. Keep in mind that you will probably not have the final say in parenting issues, even if your husband is your ally, A custodial mother usually holds the trump card, but that's no reason for a stepmother to give up.

One stepmother learned that her stepdaughter was not allowed (or that was the gist of things, details often being unclear or missing in stepmothering situations) to have a party at her home. This struck a sympathetic chord in this stepmother because she had always felt unable to entertain in her own home as a teenager, and she believed that her stepdaughter should have that opportunity. So she and her husband arranged to give a cookout for her.

This gesture was not part of a contest that the stepmother was waging with the girl's mother. It was something the stepmother thought she could do for her stepdaughter that apparently her mother, at the time, did not.

BAD MOTHERS

Some issues between ex and step go a lot deeper than giving parties. "I have stood by and watched Bruce's ex-wife use that boy as a tool against his father until he has been totally crippled," remarked a stepmother who said of their ex-wife, "I hate her guts." Her bile increases when she talks about her stepson's learning disability. According to the stepmother, she spotted it first, but his natural mother refused to recognize it or have him examined for five years. Finally, the stepmother threatened to take him to a doctor herself. Eventually, her husband did, and the boy's problem was diagnosed and treated. "What kind of mother would do that?" asked his stepmother. Other women ask the same question when their stepchildren arrive with holes in their underwear or without a toothbrush.

Stepmothers often have trouble reconciling their hatred for their husband's ex-wife with their love for their husband. "Don't you wonder how this sweet and wonderful man you married could have been married to a horror like her?" asked one stepmother.

One thing is certain. A slipshod mother goes a long way toward dispelling the cruel-stepmother myth. "I have such little respect for the mother that I don't see myself as the wicked stepmother at all," said the stepmother of an eight-year-old, who reckons, "My stepdaughter needs some strong, solid female figure around. That's me."

I suspect that all things considered, most second wives would prefer that their predecessor be an admirable individual, partly to avoid the uncomfortable quandary over how their husband could have loved two such different women, and also because an equal rival, if rivalry is the point, says more about you than a pushover matchup against a frump. She elevates the league you're playing in. Most stepmothers do give credit where it's due. Sisterhood has raised everyone's consciousness. Stepmothers will often show sympathy for an ex-wife's adjustment or for her problems as a single parent.

Of course, empathy and goodwill are in greater evidence when both women's lives are going well, and it is easier for an ex-wife to feel benevolent if her life is running smoothly. Ex-wives may have wounds to lick and pieces to pick up before they can welcome their ex-husband's happy new marriage, regardless of who initiated their divorce. The best ex-and-step relationships require sensitivity and caution.

One stepmother who reviled her ex-wife's conduct and commonly referred to her in expletives showed a sudden flash of empathy when she considered her ex's motives. "She was stuck behind with the kids. She saw her husband go off and have a happy new life. She'll never forgive and she'll never forget. I'd feel the same way. My husband did her wrong, even if it was out of ignorance. I can't guarantee that I'd act better in her shoes." Going one step further, she conceded, "I give her credit about the kids. They are moral and polite children. That's mostly her influence. My husband wasn't there." Then why the venom and and hatred? "She's a sponge on us now and an intrusion on my territory."

FACE-TO-FACE ENCOUNTERS

Encounters between ex-wife and stepmother are invariably awkward for both women. Betsy, a stepmother, was introduced around at her stepson's soccer match by his mother, also known by the same last name. So Mrs. X introduced Mrs. X. Betsy said, "It made me feel creepy."

The best reason for cooperation between stepmother and ex-wife is that it's in the interests of the children. There's a nice ironic twist to the fact that in times when people no longer stay married for the sake of the children, former and current wives might create a tentative peace for the youngsters' sake. I don't want to stretch the sisterhood notion too far, but women who manage this kind of alliance do a service to the notion of women as the enlightened, peace-minded sex with higher regard for emotional and human values. Such cooperation can soothe family relationships and minimize the destructive effects of divorce on families.

Over the last ten years I have heard of an increasing number of stepfamilies in which the biological mother and the step-mother routinely get together for certain inclusive holiday celebrations. The longer the relationship continues, the easier it gets. In one instance a woman and her husband's ex-wife work out the cross-country visitation details for her two stepchildren because the exes have so much trouble communicating. "It always breaks down into some power and control thing, so his ex and I just calmly work it out," says the stepmother.

A stepmother of twenty years tells me that she genuinely enjoys the birthday dinners for her stepchildren that she, her husband, her stepchildren, and their children spend together with her husband's ex-wife and her husband at their house. "It is so great for the kids. I like that it's a family occasion for the kids that is not on our turf and it has made ties that bind us all together over the years. My children know their stepsiblings' mother and their father's first wife. She's not a mystery, and she is a gracious hostess and wonderful cook, which makes it very nice for me," says the stepmother.

If all this chumminess is anathema to a stepmother, she doesn't have to do it. These relationships are nothing if not optional. Expressing an honest preference is advisable, according to professionals. "There should be a lot of open discussion in these situations," maintains Eric Riss, Ph.D., head of the Institute for the Exploration of Marriage of New York, who believes there is no reason that former and current wives cannot cooperate and attend the same social events—if everyone agrees. I'd like to add that I don't think ex-wives have the right to ban stepmothers from places or occasions. Perhaps exes who don't wish to encounter their husband's new wife should decide to stay home.

Nobody says you have to embrace at the head table, but ridiculous skittishness, such as is exhibited by ex-wives who develop the vapors if a stepmother is sitting in the car that drops their children at home, creates more foolishness than a step-mother should have to bear.

The best a stepmother can hope for is a healthy outlook of her own in these trying situations. Though there is sometimes comedy here, it is black comedy, and a stepmother who is deal-ing with a living ex-wife has to do her best not to get drawn into that woman's neuroses. One stepmother insisted that she and her husband move from their community because the ex-wife was watching her constantly. The ex had refused the stepmother's invitation to meet face to face, but she made cer-tain the stepmother knew that she had been under observation by telling her children and ex-husband about it. This ex-wife's neurotic behavior influenced everyone's thinking and conduct. It was an unspoken rule that the stepmother should not be with her husband when he dropped his kids home at the end of the weekend. One Sunday he decided to break the rule. That day in the car, the stepmother, who is no shrinking violet, recalled, "When we turned down the street, my legs were like jelly." Her stepson cried out, "'Dad, what are you doing?" True to form, the ex-wife came to the door and announced to her children: "Say goodbye to your father. You won't be seeing him next weekend."

It was obviously high time that the three adults took hold of an unhealthy situation. The stepmother, feeling powerless and demeaned, lobbied for a professional intermediary. Not surpris-ingly, the stepson, caught in so much crossfire, ended up shortly thereafter with a child psychologist, who insisted that all three parents come together for a visit to break the ice. Once the ex and the stepmother met face to face, both women's neuroses and anxieties dissipated. Today they even work out travel arrange-ments over the phone.

Stepmothers and ex-wives have a right to be curious about

one another. "My husband built up his ex as an ogre, and I needed to see her for myself," said a stepmother who had occasion to meet the husband's ex-wife when her stepdaughter urged the two to get together. After their meeting, she said, "This woman became a reasonable human being in my thinking, even if she'd been bad for my husband." But if an ex-wife refuses, there's not much you can do. One stepmother, who for logistical reasons must be the one who picks up her stepdaughter every Friday, goes to the ex-wife's house and rings the doorbell, then returns to the car until her stepdaughter comes out of the house. "Her mother looks like a lunatic for requiring this, but I just don't let it get to me. When Megin climbs in the car, we start talking about something else. There's nothing else we can do," she remarked.

A stepmother can't escape some conditions that ex-wives pose. If an ex is mentally or physically ill, a stepmother may have to tackle the task of shoring up a child to deal with sad or tragic circumstances. Many stepmothers talk of making excuses to their stepchildren for their mother.

"My stepson's mother refuses to drive him to the bus station when he's coming to our house. It's so petty and awkward. He is always upset. We usually pay for a taxi, or he walks. I think his mother needs a boot in the rear, but I don't say that. I've tried to explain to him that she's just having trouble coping with the new arrangement, that she doesn't mean to hurt him," a stepmother said. Another stepmother gives her five-year-old custodial stepdaughter a birthday present every year and says that it has arrived from her mother, who always forgets. Kindly assurance that helps a child handle his or her mother's ugly behavior or neglect is in order from a stepmother, but family professionals say you don't have to go overboard. For instance, a bogus birthday present isn't necessary. A simple explanation about a mother's troubles that can smooth over her omission or bad conduct is sufficient from you. Your objective should be to comfort the child, not absolve the mother. Children invariably know and sense their parents' weaknesses. They'll know if you try to cover up. What they will appreciate is positivism and kindness.

When stepchildren are handicapped or have severe behavior problems, everyone profits if a stepmother and ex-wife cooperate. Needless to say, a stepmother has much to gain in her husband's estimation if she can rise to this occasion, but many ex-wives flunk on their end. One stepmother who has a badly retarded stepdaughter finally gave up trying to get advice and guidance from the mother, who insists the child will be able to lead a normal life. She circumvented the whole trying relationship by turning to a doctor for advice.

A stepmother has to moderate her reactions to her ex-wife's behavior, for her own stability as much as for the good of the children. Whatever your opinion is, don't malign their mother to the children. Though making a face or rolling your eyes at her unreasonableness is forgivable, an outright attack on her also challenges the children's integrity. They will always identify to some degree with their biological mother.

Though it's tempting to make the ex-wife the scapegoat for your stepparenting hassles, it's usually unconstructive to do so. Even if she is at fault, you can't change her, and if you allow yourself to become obsessed with hatred for her, then you have to carry the sting of such feelings in yourself. Automatically blaming her for your woes also prevents you from facing and overcoming your own shortcomings and makes less certain the kind of personal growth many stepmothers achieve as they cope with their situations. Find a way to live with her, as you would an allergy. It's likely to flare up from time to time, but you know how to treat yourself. Unless she moves to the moon or marries a mogul, as the mother of your stepchildren, she's going to continue to figure in your life somehow.

Fortunately, the size and effect of her role in your life depends largely on you. This may be one area of stepmothering where high expectations for yourself are in order. It's hard to be impeccable, but most stepmothers would rather be some model of tolerance and show their stepchildren that they care enough for them not to put them in awkward positions just to score points against their mother. Give the ex every chance to cooperate in the present, and if she fails, make damn sure that she remains a relic of a clearly bygone past. That is within your power.

ivorce accounts for most stepmothering, but when a husband was widowed before marriage or his ex has died since, a stepmother faces different problems and considerations. Though his ex-wife is not an actual presence, her memory may be more formidable to reckon with.

Stepchildren whose mother died after their father remarried have special problems because they don't have a parent to share their grief. The remarried husband, though saddened, has not lost a spouse as they have lost a parent. In cases where the natural mother died before the father's remarriage, stepmothers often get involved subsequently in the child's grief and mourn the natural mother, too. Many inexplicable emotions commonly cause such stepmothers to feel adrift. A professional may be best suited to helping them decipher their feelings, and to guiding a child—and perhaps a husband—through the important process of grieving and adjusting.

One stepmother who married a widower found it was she who burst into tears and fell into depressions when she ran across endearing notes and chatty cooking instructions written to her stepchildren by their dead mother. "I was drawn into sadness," she recalled. "I underestimated the period of adjustment I would have to make."

A stepmother of children whose mother is dead must take care to allow her stepchildren their memories. When their mother is living, you assume the children can mostly discuss and express affection for her outside your home and company. But when a mother is dead, and if the children live with you, you cannot deny them their right and need to refer to her.

Some women may think that a mother who is dead quickly recedes into the past and may be easier to abide than a living mother. In fact, the opposite may be true. Even a dead ex-wife cannot be snuffed out of your life. Her children no longer have the real object of their affection, so they will need to integrate her memory and influence into their current lives.

Experts say that remarriages without an ex-wife to contend with do have an easier time overall. The marriage benefits. However, the children are another story. They experience a greater sense of loss and conflicting loyalties than they would if their mother were living. They worry that their father's new marriage negates their mother, and even suggests that perhaps she was never loved. So they often vow to remain loyal to her, to tend her flame. Obviously, a stepmother in these situations is going to have difficulty.

There are several things to keep in mind. If your husband and stepchildren cling to the way their life used to be—"like Mom did it" or "My wife used to"—they have not properly grieved or broken with their past. "After I married my husband, I was the one who had to throw his former wife's old perfume bottles out of the medicine chest. He had never been able to do it," said a stepmother who came to realize that the shadow of her predecessor was mostly the result of her new family's inability to accept her death.

Signs of mourning hurt and disturb a stepmother, who is made to feel like an outsider in her own house. She may worry that her husband remarried in confusion and that his commitment to her is as uncertain as his belief that his grieving had ended. These troubling suggestions don't need to be danger signs for marriage if you know how to react.

Make a concerted effort to get your husband and his children some counseling from a church, community, or professional group or counselor who addresses the effects of death on a family. Discussing their loss and confusion usually provides great relief and help. If your position amid this process—one that you cannot really be a part of—challenges your security and well-being, talking to someone outside your family who's been through the same experience can help. Think of this period as temporary, a lull in your marriage and future family life—not a threat or personal offense.

Widowed men—and their children—are often eager to reconstruct a happy new life, but their desire may precede their emotional readiness. The nagging inability to move into the future without dragging along the past may not become evident until after the marriage, when new and old sentiments pull a husband and his children in conflicting directions.

Though it's natural to feel somewhat threatened and resentful in these situations, you can help your new family members to work through their lingering grief and mourning with patience and understanding. You can help them recognize, admit, and discuss their grief. Your feelings are secondary, but it's all right to mention them and to serve as a reminder that your common goal is to move forward as a family into the future.

Don't set yourself up in competition with their mother's memory. Your role and her role in their lives are distinctly different. They may see them as unrelated, so don't make the connection in your own mind. Remember that their grief is not a rejection of you. The stepmother who opposes her stepchildren's mourning of their mother, a natural and necessary reaction, needlessly wrongs herself.

However, because your position in regard to the children's dead mother suggests competition with her memory, your stepchildren may distrust your concern and intervention in their grief. You may need to stand aside. Also, be careful not to overburden yourself with an in-depth study of your husband's ex-wife and past relationship. Knowing too much always invites comparison and tends to make you romanticize the past. Ask as much about her and his lingering grief as is necessary to move ahead with confidence in your new family relationships, but consider yourself a beacon for your new family's future, not a probe of the past. Their mother will never live in your mind as she does in theirs, so look forward instead of back. That, after all, is where your interests lie.

I heard of a family in which the mother, who knew that she

had a terminal disease, brought in a consultant to begin helping her husband and their children adjust to her imminent death. Their mourning was complete when her husband remarried several years later. The children's new stepmother said, "They have never made me feel as if I challenge their mother in any way. They really knew what their relationship with her was about and what her loss meant to them. Their having those things has given me the chance to be myself and to make what I can of our relationships."

Family psychologists have examined the effect of a former spouse's death on remarriage. They caution families against making the former wife into a family saint. It's easier to remember a living ex-wife's faults or frailties than a dead mother's. She tends to be idealized, which plainly drives a stepmother crazy. "I want my stepchildren to have fond memories, but I feel as if I'm in a no-win situation with them. I am not and cannot be their mother, and they remember the one they had as perfect. I always feel like second best, drab and ordinary, next to her memory," observed a stepmother.

Another stepmother said, "I never feel dogged by her memory because I don't compete to be their mother. I think that they are lucky to have someone else to care for and about them now. I can't be their mom, but I am something very good and extra in their lives since she died."

Your husband, in-laws, and other family members can often help you escape the sainted memory of a former wife. Learning more about her from those who do not revere her, as children often do, can do you a world of good. "My sister-in-law gave me a realistic picture of my husband's first wife. She didn't badmouth her, but it was nice to learn that she had some faults that her children don't remember," stated one woman. You will probably have to bring up the subject. Most people assume that you're sensitive to hearing about a first wife and politely try not to mention her.

Stepmothers typically try to replace their stepchildren's dead mother. Even if you don't actually want the full responsibility of mothering, you may feel it is your duty to swoop in and become a mother hen—to be the heroine of the situation. Your stepchildren may be delighted to have a new mother figure—someone to put some maternal touches on their lives—but they realize that you can't automatically become their mother. Take things slowly for your sake and theirs. Stepchildren are not your children. You may be an unrivaled maternal influence in their lives now, and you are certainly an immediate presence—but you're not their mother and they won't forget that.

Since stepchildren often feel disloyal to their mother's memory when they accept care and affection from someone else in her role, make things easier for them by telling them that you won't pretend to be their mother, that you don't wish to cancel out her memory. Mention her from time to time to show them that you keep her in mind and are big enough to live with reality. Chances are you'll get along better with them.

OLD FRIENDS

Former friends of your husband and his ex-wife can also have expectations that can be trying for a new stepmother who has married a widower. They often expect the second wife to be a copy of the first. I was taken aback at the way a couple of some experience and sophistication discussed the new wife of a widowed good friend. The man had two older teenage sons when his first wife died. Three years later he married a woman seven years his junior whom his friends considered unlike his first wife. She was a poor choice "to mother the boys," in their opinion. They were hoping for someone who could be a stand-in for the first wife, a replacement mother. As I listened, I wondered how they could be naïve enough to expect a man of forty to marry again with the intent to provide a mother for his children, especially when his children were almost grown. They gave little or no consideration to what their friend may have been seeking in a new partner or to the impossibility that any stepmother could step into the real mother's shoes. A stepmother under the pressure of such expectations might ask her husband to have a gentle confidence with his old friends about what is reasonable to expect from a stepmother. He might want to include some of the reasons he chose to marry her so his friends may begin to appreciate the new union, too. This story was a reminder that it is healthy, and probably wise, for a stepmother and her husband to make new friends as well as preserve some of the old in order to keep from living in the shadow of the dead.

THEIR MOTHER'S BELONGINGS

Stepchildren feel entitled to things that belonged to their mother and they often feel that a stepmother threatens their right to them. It's best if the matter can be settled before your wedding. If your husband has not considered this, you should ask him to.

One stepmother-to-be was appalled when her future husband invited her and his grown children over to sort through his dead wife's personal belongings a week before their wedding. "I think he saw it as a ritual, best done before his marriage, but to the rest of us it seemed as if he was saying, 'Last chance. Come and get it before your stepmother takes over.' They were uncomfortable that I was there at all. It was handled badly."

Sorting through a mother's things should be done well before a father's second wedding, and it's best if you are not involved. If your husband wishes to reserve something special to give you, he should do it on his own and leave you out of his negotiations and conversations with his children. It's important that you do not appear to be taking her things away from them.

It is also his place to offer them the personal items—jewelry, clothing, and so forth—left by their mother. If he doesn't or hasn't by the time you are on the scene, you can. Most second wives want to disassociate themselves from a first wife's possessions, but be careful not to make one serious mistake: don't dispose of anything until you've consulted the children. The brooch or hat that seems worthless to you may mean something to the children, so give them the chance to refuse it.

All children enjoy heirlooms and the bit of a parent's history that they represent. If your stepchildren are very young, pack away a few things to give them later. They'll appreciate it.

A father is also well advised to discuss with older children the changes in his will and their inheritance brought about by his remarriage. It is always better that he talk openly with them about his decisions and reasoning. There is no reason for them to be kept in the dark and be surprised later. Remarried couples should consult a lawyer for help in redistributing their assets fairly. A dead mother's share, if it's earmarked for the children, should be set aside early in a remarriage to avoid confusion or bitterness later. Though such precautions may sound overconscientious at the start of a marriage, money and inheritance can become sticky issues later and should be prepared for early.

Keeping stepchildren informed about their inheritance will

also prevent confusion later if you should outlive your husband and execute his estate. It's crucial that the children know that financial matters have been arranged to suit his wishes. Now that their mother is dead, they may feel left without an advocate in such matters, and it's important that their father settle their uncertainties.

A dead mother can be a lot for a stepmother to reckon with. Try hard to regard her realistically and not to be threatened by the past. No stepmother should compete in the mothering department.

7

The Remarried Ex-Wife

ecause your stepchildren's mother is such an integral part of your stepfamily, her fortunes matter more than you might suppose. If she is unhappy or needy, you are likely to know about it. If her circumstances are unpleasant, even if she has brought them upon herself, she may tug on your conscience.

Her presence is felt most if she is unmarried and relies on your husband for financial support. Her alimony may be a chunk out of your new household's budget. Furthermore, even if she receives little financial support, you may still catch yourself comparing your life to hers, feeling guilty if she is needy or feeling short if you are strapped on her account. One stepmother stated, "My husband and I always worried that at the time we became solvent, his kids would step forward with tears in their eyes and tell us their mother was eating roots to live." The way some ex-wives act, some stepmothers would be able to sleep in peace no matter what the ex had to eat, but others among us have more sensitive consciences.

It's easy to see why an ex-wife's remarriage is so universally hoped for and welcomed. "I never knew how much she figured into my life until I felt how relieved I was when she got married. It meant no more guilt or obligations on my husband's part. She was finally going to have her own life and be out of ours. I felt totally exhilarated," one stepmother said.

An ex-wife's remarriage usually means many positive things for a stepmother. Her emotional and financial dependence sometimes end. Remarriage suggests that an ex-wife has found happiness and that she no longer lives in the shadow of you and your husband, or as a satellite to your marriage. It ends the *haves* (you and your husband) and *have-nots* (her) pattern that exists in many stepfamilies.

The relationship between a stepmother and an ex-wife usually takes on a different, more relaxed, and more balanced character after the ex-wife remarries. If a civilized relationship is likely between the two women, remarriage will usually help it along. Jealousies and competition are put to rest. It's easier for an ex-wife to deal with you if her own life is settled and she feels on equal terms. Assuming that the marriage is a happy one, she may feel better in general and less defensive about protecting her rights with her children and ex-husband.

The positive features of an ex-wife's remarriage are those that usually spring to mind for you and your husband. To the two of you, her remarriage may seem a godsend. But it's a more complicated emotional matter for your stepchildren.

Though they, too, may be pleased—even relieved—to see their mother find a new partner and new direction in life, her remarriage is more likely to unsettle their lives. Children who live with their mother must adjust to a stepfather, and perhaps a new house, neighborhood, or room arrangement. They may also feel in competition for their mother's attention and affection—all the same things they felt about their father when he married you. A stepmother should understand that it's a tough time for them.

"My stepson was in boarding school when his mother announced her plans to remarry. He knew and liked the guy she was marrying, but he told us that he'd begun to dream about his house being gone when he went home for Christmas. He felt threatened and displaced," a stepmother related. Suddenly she could see remarriage and its effect on kids from the outside.

There are certain subtle things that you can do to help. You and your husband will want to reassure a child that his or her place in your home remains the same. A child shouldn't think that his mother's remarriage will in any way endanger his relationship with his father. He or she may even rely more on you for constancy while the conditions in his own home are in flux.

A stepfather may also threaten your husband if this new man in your extended family becomes a rival for your stepchildren's affection. If the children will live with this new man, your husband may feel jealous of the time and influence he will have in their lives. A period of adjustment is necessary for everybody.

Sometimes a mother's attitude toward her children changes

with remarriage. She may find children a liability to her new marriage and lose interest in caring for them. Some remarried mothers decide to give custody to their ex-husband. In addition to the logistical problems that this turn of events causes step-mothers, it is an enormously difficult period for children. You and your husband may need to be on hand to support and help a child to adjust. For your part, try to create a welcoming atmos-phere that doesn't capitalize on the child's loss to endear your-self to him or her, and don't make the mother out to be a villain. The child is having a tough enough time coping with his own anger and loss without adding the need to defend his mother.

Helping your stepchild to make these adjustments can only help the relationship that the two of you will form together later. Some mature insight about this transition time and the feelings your stepchild and his mother are experiencing are the best you can offer him. This would also be a good time to offer a camp-ing trip or ski weekend—or another special and distracting activ-ity to boost a child's independence and self-esteem. Some extra time together and the concern that you and your husband show reaffirm your stepchild's tie with his father and you.

Even adult children react noticeably when a parent remarries. A family of four adult women I know brooded when they thought that the chances of their mother's remarrying were slim. They didn't want to be responsible for her in their adult lives. But when she finally decided to marry, you would have thought she'd personally offended them. The eldest, a mother herself, worried about where her young children would spend the Christmas holidays. The youngest daughter, still single, resented being the "old maid" of the family. She also confessed that to her the act signified the end of her old family. "First we lost Dad and now Mom," she remarked. Their mother's remarriage had wide-ranging real and emotional significance for everybody.

Being aware of and sympathetic to your stepchildren's problems needn't diminish the relief and happiness that you feel over their mother's remarriage. You can revel in it silently. Sing a sweet chorus of hallelujahs in the shower.

ow we come to the root of this ruckus: the stepchildren. Having your mind and your marriage in order is only part of the story. The children are the rest of it—and the most unpredictable. They ultimately make stepmothering worthwhile or worthless, bearable or beastly.

Stepchildren have their own special ways, intentional or not, of making stepmothers feel like outsiders. "My stepson acts as if I'm not here. When he talks to his dad, he's superanimated, fun, lively. But his conversations with me are strictly perfunctory. His eyes glaze over—if he looks my way at all," said a woman who is baffled by how unnatural she feels in his presence. The one-sided nature of their conversations also aggravates her. "I know all about his school marks, hobbies, pets, even the star pitchers on his favorite baseball teams. But I don't think he's ever asked me the time of day about myself."

This imbalance is built in to stepmothering, partly because adults are less self-centered and also because a child and his father who don't live together are busy compressing their relationship into a short period of time. There's a lot for them to catch up on, and a child undoubtedly has some parental attention coming.

When these one-sided conversations become the rule, a father should certainly try to involve his wife, even discuss the pattern with his child, who probably is aware of what he's doing, if not exactly why. Ignoring a stepmother, like not looking her in the eye, is a child's way of saying that he hasn't yet accepted her and this marriage. He'd rather she weren't there. Given time, most kids do come around, but the waiting period is difficult for stepmothers. While you wait, write letters in your head or draw up your Christmas list. Give the impression that you've come to stay. But don't plead for attention, and even more important, *don't give a stepchild the opportunity to rebuff you.* Restraint is difficult when you're anxious for these relations to improve, but if you get into emotional debt with a stepchild, it's hard to get out. It's unlikely that he or she will make it up to you.

It helps to understand what stepchildren are thinking about in their relationship with you. They are less likely to take your position into account, so it's to your advantage to understand theirs. You don't have to sacrifice your own interests on a stepchild's behalf, but some knowledge of why they act and feel as they do can prevent you from inadvertently making mistakes or expecting too much from them. Your sensitivity and ability to take your stepchild's predicament into consideration will help both of you.

ROCKING THE BOAT

Stepchildren have usually been through an ordeal: their parents' divorce. Like most survivors of a trauma, they don't want to suffer anymore, and they want to get beyond the difficult past. Like scorned lovers, they shy away from new personal involvements and seem preoccupied with their own interests. Their reserve can be discouraging and unnerving for stepmothers.

Several factors are at work in their psyches. Stepchildren warm to a stepmother slowly. Because they have witnessed the disintegration of their parents' marriage, they want to avoid experiencing a sense of loss again. They withhold affection, even from persons they may be drawn to and like, until they can sense and see that the new person's presence is permanent and worth their effort. Psychologists say the reaction is usually unconscious, a simple self-protective impulse. It is another reason a stepmother should convey a sense of confidence and positivism to her stepchildren instead of seeming to wait for their approval. Her relationship to them depends a lot on their acceptance, but her relationship to their father does not. They should get that message.

Another common trait among stepchildren is their intolerance of, and obvious discomfort with, discord. They will go to almost any length to avoid quarrels and dissension of any kind. One stepmother who was getting along well with her stepdaughter on a sailing trip felt a definite iciness between them when she remarked that the girl's mother was childish to demand that only her father be in the car when she was driven home. "I think my stepdaughter agreed with my opinion, but she couldn't handle any wrangling or hostility between adults. She wants everything to be peaceful, calm. She tenses at the suggestion of an argument. I think she feels that she's lost enough already to adult differences," the stepmother said.

Older stepchildren, teens or adults, who are not as defenseless as younger children, can argue with a parent's terms or fight for a principle, but younger stepchildren are usually unable or unwilling to do so. They simply want peace and pleasantness. They don't want you to rock the boat anymore. When voices are raised or tempers flare, they withdraw into themselves until any emotional storm passes over them.

Furthermore, you and their father may have a confrontational and conversational style that is different from what they are familiar with. One stepmother reported: "My husband and I have some real dustups. They're just part of our relationship. We kiss and make up within the hour usually, but first we shout and snarl at each other. He says he and his ex-wife never did that except during their breakup. When his son is staying with us and we bicker over taking out the trash or who left the bike in the driveway, I can see my stepson go into agony. So we've tried to keep it down for his sake. Sometimes I tell him after a spat that everything is okay—he can come out now."

A QUESTION OF STYLE

Stepchildren have another problem similar to their stepmother's discomfort at entering a different family with established habits, history, and rules. A college junior, a stepchild, told of the adjustment she had to make to her stepmother. "My mom is not very

demonstrative. She's low-key, reserved. She also dresses very con-
servatively. Then here comes my dad and stepmother on parents'
weekend. She's got on sunglasses, a fur coat, and makeup. She
likes to hug and kiss us. At first I was horrified. I didn't want my
friends to think she was my mother. She's okay to have a good
time with, but she's not my mother. It's taken me a while to get
used to her, not to be embarrassed. My friends actually like her.
But she's different from us." That says a lot.

You may not think of yourself as an Auntie Mame sort of
character, but to timid stepchildren that may be the way you
come across. If they're a flamboyant clan, you may seem to be the
quiet one. Sometimes you're just different. It takes some getting
used to, especially for kids who have less experience meeting and
dealing with a cross section of different people than adults do.

You shouldn't have to act out of character with your stepchildren, but you can play down your differences if you are hoping
to blend in. At least understand their early discomfort with you.

HOME AWAY FROM HOME

A change in the place where a stepchild lives, visits, or returns
also requires an adjustment for him. Children in general tend to
be conservative toward changes. A teenage stepdaughter whose
stepmother remodeled the house that her dead mother had
originally decorated remembers being extremely unsettled by
the changes. "I came home from camp, and every trace of my
mother was gone. I cried and cried. First I had to get used to my
stepmother, but why did she change our house?" The stepmother obviously had some rights of her own to make changes,
but they came as a jolt to her stepdaughter, who initially
regarded them as hostile acts. The transition would have been

easier for her if she'd been around and helped to feel that she was part of the process. Such little things as choosing a room color or seeing a floor plan can help make a child feel part of the changing process instead of a victim of it.

To a stepmother's frequent surprise, adult stepchildren also react negatively to household and style changes, "My stepchildren are clearly grown-ups, but they don't like to come to our house, I know," a stepmother said. "It's not their place or home. It's not how they'd do it. Our style is different from their old home, and I think they resent not having an old homestead." This woman dauntlessly tried to make some gesture to the more obviously troubled of her stepdaughters, to signal that she understood and sympathized with her loss and feelings. So she dug up all the old family photos of the former family home and arranged them for her in a scrapbook. "She was entitled to them, and I hoped it would help," the stepmother stated. She can't be sure it didn't. If you think things happen quickly with stepchildren, reconsider. Two years later the stepmother was thanked for sending the album. "She told me it meant a lot to her, but she obviously wasn't able to say it or reckon with the subject for that long," she noted.

Another reality for stepchild-stepmother relations is that children and adolescents perceive things differently than they do later as adults. There's no way to avoid some of stepmothering's more hazardous aspects completely. A thirty-three-year-old stepchild said, "I look back now, and I can see that I was perfectly awful to my stepmother. I hated her. I never stopped to think that my dad loved her or that she had a life. I did everything I could to punish her for not being my mother. Now I see her position differently, but when I was thirteen, there was no way I could do that. She was my nemesis." A stepmother can acquit herself honorably with such a child and protect herself from repeated injury only by knowing what she's up against. It would hardly be advisable for her to pretend that they're the best of friends or to be crushed if she's forgotten on Mother's Day.

A child's side of stepfamily life can be grim, unfortunately. You don't always know what is happening or what stepchildren are hearing in their home if they don't live with you. "We found out later that their mother told them I was the reason their father and she divorced. I didn't even know him when they separated," asserted a stepmother. It's a frequently heard story. Some mothers punish children who visit their father or make them promise not to befriend or like their stepmother. One stepmother was disgusted to learn that her stepson was required to report every detail of his visit, down to the color of her clothes, as soon as he returned home. "I'm sure he found it extremely unpleasant," she said.

Reported one new stepmother, "I used to laugh at how ridiculous some of the things my husband's ex-wife told the kids sounded, but when I saw the tears and looks on their faces for myself, I finally knew what they were going through." In her case, her stepchildren's mother made her two daughters swear never to kiss or hug their stepmother. The night before the girls' visit with her and their father ended, the promise slipped out. "We had always hugged and kissed goodbye before, and they were very troubled by what saying goodbye the next day was going to be like. They wanted to talk it over," she stated.

The oldest girl said that she would respect her mother's wishes not to kiss her stepmother, but she wanted her to know that she cared as much for her. "We'd never talked about affection before. It was very emotional. Suddenly all this stuff wasn't ridiculous. There sat the three of us crying with emotion. Their mother would have died. I'm sure it wasn't what she had in mind," she remarked.

Sometimes a child's difficulties at home aren't attempts on the mother's part to sabotage a stepmother, but they are true crises that unsettle a child and make forming a relationship with a stepmother difficult anyway. "I sat by my mother's side twice after she tried to kill herself," said a stepchild who felt unable to respond warmly or normally to his stepmother. His emotional circuits were already overloaded.

AGE DIFFERENCES

The age of stepchildren greatly affects their reaction to their father's remarriage and stepmother. Women who are inexperienced with children and their stages of development should do a little elementary research to help them make the most of things—or protect themselves.

Babies and toddlers require the most physical attention, but are generally more responsive and affectionate than older children. Toddlers like routine and need to be told repeatedly about plans that involve them because they do not yet comprehend the concept of time. Color in the days on the calendar that children will be staying with you to help them understand the length of a visit. Clearly convey your pleasure when you see them. They will usually respond.

Those tips are from experts who find that preschoolers can move back and forth between two households quite easily if parents cooperate. "They enjoy spending time with both families; they think that this is just the way the world is," say counselors Emily and John Visher.

Young children, four to ten, may be the easiest group for a

stepmother. They can express their thoughts and feelings, yet they are not as physically demanding as toddlers. Accustomed to changes in teachers, classrooms, and classmates, they usually are more adaptive by nature and easier to please. Less encumbered by guilt and loyalty to their mother than adolescents may be, they are also responsive to a warm, family-type atmosphere. "The younger child is more apt to be trustful and accepting than the older child, who must sever bonds of loyalty to the absent parent," states Lucille Duberman, a sociologist and assistant professor at Rutgers University. Experts stress the need to talk honestly and directly with children of all ages, but children from four to ten need special help in handling their emotions. This age group needs to be told that feelings and behavior are two separate things. You and their father can convey that you understand and accept their feelings about you and their father's new life, while at the same time they may need to control and to learn new behavior. They can feel angry with you for sharing their father, even wish you weren't around, but they cannot talk rudely or kick you in the shins, for instance.

A stepmother may need to extend her patience and understanding with children who are only beginning to learn about controlling their emotions. This age group also needs to be told about plans that affect them, such as trips, visits, and school changes, well in advance when possible. Kids adapt very well when they're given fair warning, so don't keep them in the dark about events that concern them.

Adolescents are the worst for a stepmother because they suffer the most. They push a stepmother to her limit because their aims are different. They want space and independence. "The stepmother without children of her own who marries a man with adolescents has the most difficult time of anyone," notes Dr.

John Visher. It can be murder. The children are more likely to identify with their parents and to be swayed by their opinions and loyalties. Yet they resent being caught in the middle, so they often remain aloof, less communicative, and careful. They are breaking away from parental influence and authority at this stage in their personal development anyhow. "They're less likely to be on friendly terms with their parents, whether natural or step," states Duberman. You never know exactly where you stand with them. Give them space and don't go around with your feelings on your sleeve. With adolescents it's better to come across to them as a parental figure rather than a peer, unless you're ready to be treated as irrationally as they sometimes treat each other.

A parent's remarriage usually causes a teenager to turn to friends and peers more than to parents and to break away from home relationships sooner. Of course they still need guidance, but emotionally they may shift their allegiance and involvement away from home. The trick for parents and stepparents is to understand that their children haven't abandoned them forever. Leave the door of your relations open. They will return with a fuller sense of their adult identities.

Stepfamilies with teenagers experience real hostility if parents push them to participate in new households against their will. They just can't make their own transition to a new identity with too many demands on them. You can help the situation by offering them *some* control in your household, such as plans about food and schedules—matters that help them to feel they have an active part in your home and not just duties and obligations.

SEX DIFFERENCES

The sex of stepchildren influences both their reaction to you and some of your attitudes toward them. As a rule, stepmothers find stepdaughters more difficult than stepsons. The same sexes are more likely to compete, and (like natural mothers) stepmothers have more explicit expectations about how a child of their own sex should behave. Stepdaughters, especially adolescents, may identify with their own mothers, which makes the sense of rivalry between you more acute. As you are probably already beginning to see, an adolescent stepdaughter can really make a stepmother's life interesting.

Work hard to establish yourself on an adult level and to demonstrate that you are not in competition with your stepdaughter for Daddy's affections—or anything else. The temptation most often for a stepmother of an adolescent girl is to try to be her pal. If you do not have a daughter of your own, you may transfer feelings of identity to her—expect her to dress, act, and think as you do. Stepdaughters usually don't want to be burdened with our expectations for them. They may have more than enough of their mother's to contend with. A better relationship is likely to develop between the two of you if you try not to pressure a stepdaughter to conform to your goals and standards. You're better off being a model or resource for her when she's ready to seek you out than trying to take her in hand. The latter often backfires and forces a rebellion.

A stepmother reported: "Janine was sixteen when I married her father. I thought she was a pathetic girl. She didn't know how to dress. She was too shy to look strangers in the face. She had not been taught a thing about proper manners, makeup, poise, or anything. So I tried to help. I took her shopping, planned her wardrobe, had her hair cut, and sent her to a makeup class. It took time, money, and diplomacy, but I wanted to do it. I couldn't stand to think she was my husband's daughter as she was, a casualty of his divorce." But after Janine went home with her new clothes, haircut, and new makeup know-how, her stepmother never heard a word from her. "There was not a word of thanks," she said. What was worse, when Janine visited her father and stepmother a few months later, all signs of the clothes and improvements were gone. "Her hair was oily and stringy again, she wore no makeup, and she came with nothing suitable to wear. I was so disappointed and angry that I'd wasted my time."

This kind of pattern repeats itself time and time again among stepmothers. You should make some effort to help—it may be necessary to do so to put your own mind at ease—but don't expect stepdaughters to adopt your improvements for them as though they're just what they've been waiting for. Janine's stepmother was so angry with her reaction that she stopped trying to change her appearance. Much to her surprise, Janine began to show an interest in her appearance several years later. She asked her stepmother for advice in a roundabout fashion. "'Do you think I should get my hair cut?' she asked me when she visited last summer. It was déjà vu. Hadn't we had this conversation four years ago? 'Yes, I think a good haircut would make a difference on you,' I answered casually, as though it was the first time I'd ever considered it. So she went out and had her hair cut and is paying a lot more attention to her clothes. She acts as if the very idea is new. I just shake my head. I guess she wasn't ready for help before."

Stepsons are not carefree by any means, but they are usually easier. Even when they are rebellious and difficult, as adolescent sons often may be, a stepmother seems to invest less of her emotional self in them. In fact, her sexual difference may help her to preserve some sort of communication on a male-female frequency even when father-son and other familial relationships break down. As natural mothers of sons often are, stepmothers seem to be more forgiving of stepsons.

Adolescent sons of divorce often become remote and aloof rather than overly emotional when under family pressure. They are often frightened, experts say, by the sexual attraction they may feel for a stepmother. (Keep in mind that adolescent boys are sexually attracted to just about everything.) They withdraw and are unable to express even any positive emotions toward her, though the emotions may exist just the same. Forgive them and give them time. Adolescence is hellish for everyone.

Differences in stepchildren's attitudes based on sex may exist in younger children, but they are much less noticeable. A flirty nine-year-old daddy's girl and a six-year-old boy who feels obliged to be the man of his house at too tender an age aren't uncommon personalities in remarried families, but their attitudes and personalities are more likely to be determined by their environment and upbringing, usually out of a stepmother's control.

Problems related to a child's sex usually pass as children outgrow them. For instance, stepmothers and daughters can usually become adult friends because they share more real experiences and interests. "My stepdaughter and I weren't close at all until she married a divorced man," reported one stepmother, a bit smugly. Now that the daughter is a stepmother, too, they have a lot more in common. "She tells me that I'm an example to her of how to cope," she laughed. "Now, that's a switch, isn't it?"

9

Visits

ecause so many practical, logistical, and emotional forces converge during your stepchildren's visits, serious stress and anxiety are often part of visitation for stepmothers. There's an element of surprise to these strains. Most of us are ill prepared for the double whammy of kids *and* our reaction to them.

Visitation is proof that you have married a family, not just a man. "When those kids start visiting, your fantasy of what a marriage should be won't ever come true. You are never going to have the early months to be just a couple, the way you thought it would be," said a stepmother who saw her visions of Sunday breakfasts in bed disappear when her six-year-old stepdaughter started to visit every weekend.

A stepmother shouldn't panic. Early visits are often arduous and unanticipated periods of adjustment for stepmothers. Counselors usually encourage us to help set the tone and rules for stepchildren's visits in order to avoid feeling victimized by them. That sounds simple enough, but it isn't, since stepmothers have a lot of difficulty expressing their preferences and taking charge. It doesn't come easily to them, especially to women who have no other experience with other children. Fear, uncertainty, and the desire to be liked inhibit them.

Visitation, even for a stepmother who looked forward to spending time with her stepchild after her marriage, can be disconcerting. Visits can be like a splash of cold water in the face: the real test of theory versus practice. The children actually enter your life. From afar they may have once seemed more like objects: the Children. At close (very close) range they are people with distinctive personalities, physical presences, and visitation terms attached. Visitation is the ultimate reckoning with what it means to be a stepmother. They'll be coming back for a long time. That's why they're so threatening and why visitation takes on such importance.

The term "visits" evokes the idea of a child cheerily dropping in at your invitation and convenience to say hello and show off his report card. Very often, however, visits are not casual, uplifting, easy, or welcome occasions. It seems heartless to say that your husband's children aren't always a pleasure, always welcome, but it's true—and understandable. You married a man, not his children, and you looked forward to setting up a house with him, and of making a home that reflected a twosome's shared style and attitudes. If there weren't children in that home at the outset, then stepchildren become an intrusion. So, for that matter, are natural children much of the time. It takes practice and patience for natural parents to learn to live easily with their offspring.

Living with someone else's children part-time requires an even greater adjustment. Natural parents receive immediate physical and emotional feedback in return for the problems that their children cause them. A stepmother doesn't have that built-in equalizer. She has to find her own sources of satisfaction from stepmothering. Sometimes the children themselves cannot or will not give the stepmother the kind of satisfaction she needs.

Stepmothering should not require pleasing others to the exclusion of oneself any more than any other relationship does. Women who approach it in a spirit of self-sacrifice will probably end up hating it. For a stepmother, a successful approach to visits involves a combination of good feelings about her contribution to the children and the establishment of a living situation that she can live with—even enjoy. Success at this twofold endeavor would probably be the official stepmother's prayer if there were such a thing.

THE FIRST TIME

First visits, especially, can shake up a stepmother. Her husband's account of his children will help to prepare her, but even he can't predict how they'll react to her—or how she'll react to them. In fact, they may not even resemble the happy kids with Hula-Hoops in the snapshots he's shown her, the images that inspired her fantasies about taking them along on ski trips and cookouts. Their very appearance, mannerisms, and clothing may come as a jolt if they do not reflect their father's taste and style.

If all of you have met before they visit, the happy relations you enjoyed before marriage can be misleading. A stepmother was simply Dad's date or friend before, or so it may have seemed to the child. Some children get caught up in the romance of their father's courtship and do some of the courting; but that's just a sketch out of a situation comedy and altogether different from actually taking orders from their stepmother—or making a place in their lives for her. Again and again stepmothers tell of the marvelous stepchild who courted her like mad until she actually married his father. Then the pint-sized Cupid turned into a real pill.

Most stepmothers talk about psychic exhaustion after these first visits. "The children's visits mattered so much to me and my husband. After his daughter left, we went over everything we'd all said and done, looking for meaning, for every sign of success or failure. He wondered how I read her reactions. I'd ask him if I'd done the right or wrong things. The tension was so bad that I broke down and cried with relief when she left," said a stepmother of her stepdaughter's first stay in their home.

Another woman was surprised to find that her stepson's visits always put her and her husband at odds. "Every night after he went to bed, we argued about Clark—why he didn't or did what he did and what should be done about it. I never expected he'd have that effect on us," she remarked. "He didn't just come to stay with us. His presence dominated us."

ACCEPTANCE

We often load visits with too many expectations. One of those is acceptance by our stepchildren. Another is signs of progress in our relationship to them. "I thought my stepdaughter had to accept me, that she and I had to prove we could get along and be happy or else I would be a failure and my marriage would suffer," stated a stepmother. Hers is a typical attitude. Her every visit was a test. If her stepdaughter didn't kiss her goodbye or enter into some kind of frank, personal conversation with her, this woman felt that her marriage was threatened. She equated stepmothering success with marriage success.

Such eagerness to equate her achievements as a stepmother with the happiness of her marriage can undo a woman. The two shouldn't be related, and when they are, we often become hypersensitive and grovel for acceptance, a disastrous practice with kids, who sense our insecurity.

Don't grovel. Don't buy your stepdaughter the doll she admires in the shop window or make her favorite dinner the first time she comes to your house. She won't like you any better if you do or don't. Ask any experienced stepmother. She'll know that Mommy makes the best macaroni and cheese anyhow. (And even if she doesn't, you probably won't be told yours is the best for years.)

Try, of course, to make visits pleasant and comfortable occasions for your stepchildren, but pandering to them makes them feel pressured or manipulated. It's better to test their readiness to appreciate those special gestures and favors before you do them. For your own peace of mind, don't go so far out of your way to do things that you'll feel bitter about if your stepchildren don't appreciate them. Try getting acquainted in an atmosphere of goodwill, but don't bend over backward to impress or please them.

A stepmother who knit her stepdaughter several sweaters during this "courtship" period despaired after she never saw any of them worn. "For all I know, she takes them home and gives them away," she said, feeling unappreciated. She would have felt better if she hadn't made the sweaters. "I was trying too hard. I created my own disappointments," she has since reasoned. This is the time for restraint and patience.

Rather than simply trying to win the favor of her stepchildren, a stepmother should guide them into the new world created by the relationship between her husband and herself—not try to seduce them. Special gifts, dinners, and other gestures should be the icing on the cake, not the foundation of the relationship.

PRIVATE TIME

Even the physical presence of children can require a big adjustment. "We can't make any noise or run around with our clothes off," said a stepmother who misses such freedom. There is also the new fear of interruption. Compounded with emotional strain and simple physical fatigue, often the result of small children's demands, visitation can become a sexual malady that surprises and frightens stepmothers. Almost all of them mention it.

Fortunately, the problem doesn't last; as visits become a more routine and natural aspect of remarried life, your sex life will get back to normal. Adjusting your schedule can help. "On the weekends we always made love in the morning," stated a stepmother who became extremely resentful when that practice ended. "It was the only time we didn't have to jump up and get dressed for work. And then there was nine-year-old Melanie knocking on our door. It threatened to kill our sex life on weekends." Then she and her husband made it their practice to retire for the evening earlier on Saturdays. They allow themselves extra time alone before going to bed rather than tucking Melanie in and falling into bed exhausted, as they used to do. "Whether we make love or not, we feel we have some intimacy. We can still talk as adults. I think that's what matters, and it does help our sex life."

A couple needs to set aside private time during each visit, unless it is extremely short—just a few hours. It not only helps a couple adjust their relationship to the presence of a child; it also gives partners the chance to touch base with each other during the visit, and perhaps to solve problems before they become too big. This base-touching is extremely reassuring to stepmothers, who can have difficulty being themselves when their stepchildren are around. "When the kids leave, my husband always asks me what was wrong, why I was so uptight, so different from the way I am when we're alone. What can I say?" said a stepmother, puzzled by her continuing discomfort. Mixing together time with a child and time as a couple during visits usually helps a stepmother ease into the situation.

A stepmother often becomes a catalyst for her husband and his children during visitation. His bachelor life may not have accommodated children very well. While pizza dinners and carryout Chinese meals were all right for single dads, remarried fathers typically want to strengthen their ties to their children and to share their new home—including more gracious meals and accommodations. This puts a stepmother in a peculiar position.

On the one hand, it gives her the opportunity to contribute something valuable to the relationship between her husband and his children. On the other hand, if her stepchildren don't choose to include her in the closeness, she can feel left out of the spirit she helped create. Though she sets the stage, she often feels that she doesn't belong on it. "I felt left out," said one stepmother. "The kids and my husband have a good time here, but my mission is to make things nice for them. I think the kids feel more at home when they're here than I do. I feel displaced. My only role is in the kitchen or the laundry room. If I sit down to talk with them out on the patio or in the den, things get tense." She told a familiar story.

One can imagine Norman Rockwell trying to capture the nuances of this modern family portrait. The stepmother's face would need to reflect her uncertainty and discomfort, and the children's body language would suggest a sudden and confusing inhibition. The father would be falsely cheery, trying to keep things moving, as if to say, "We're all doing fine, aren't we? Let's keep it up. Please."

A stepmother's relationship with her stepchild may progress quite slowly. Only time can put an end to the strains and falseness both of you are likely to feel at first. Also, a stepmother is more likely to be the superior conversationalist and to be able to ask the questions that will draw out her stepchild. Yet she may feel left out when the stepchild shows no reciprocal interest (or the social skills to fake it) in her. Most stepmothers tell of endless dinners or car rides spent listening to accounts of team tryouts, teacher impersonations, and report card narrations. The conversation never swerves in her direction or leaves an entry for her.

SELF-DEFENSE

Visitations put children in an awkward situation, too. Their role is in some ways no more clearly defined than a stepmother's in terms of ambiguity and uncertainty about their relationship to her and to their father. They often feel victimized and powerless. A stepmother can usually somehow correct conditions that threaten her, but children usually cannot. They may be able to defend themselves in other ways, such as not looking her in the face or insulting her macaroni and cheese, or playing for Daddy's undivided attention; but they cannot genuinely affect the situation. They can only respond to it. I read a touching account, told by a therapist, of a child who traveled between his parents by train on weekends. His journey, on the "transition train," was a time in which he would prepare for the atmosphere of the next household. He often withdrew emotionally during the final hours at either place in order to make saying goodbye easier. In another case, a stepson always managed to pick an argument with his stepmother before he left. If he was angry, it was easier for him to say goodbye, to be glad to be going home.

"Stepchildren hold membership in two households," says the counseling team of Emily and John Visher, who explain that the emotional adjustment involved in shuttling back and forth often causes unpredictable behavior. The differences between those households are sometimes glaring. One stepmother was astonished and immediately sympathetic when her ten-year-old stepson, in apparent emotional anguish, begged her, "Don't make me choose what to have for dinner, please." She always gave him several choices, intended as a treat. He was not given such choices in his home, a more tightly structured household. His stepmother remarked, "It's easy to forget how differently we live, how much he must stretch to get along in both places."

The Visher team offers some tips for easing stepchildren into visitation. It can be helpful if they have some place in the household that is their own—for example, a drawer or a shelf for toys and clothes. If they are included in stepfamily chores and projects when they are with the stepfamily, they tend to feel more connected to the group. Bringing a friend with them to share the visit and having you or your husband actively participate in getting acquainted with the neighborhood can make a difference to many visiting children. Neighborhood activities such as block fairs, yard sales, and school carnivals are ways for a child to enjoy and to become accustomed to his parent's community. Knowing ahead of time that there is going to be an interesting activity—a picnic, movie, or stepfamily game of Monopoly, etc.—can sometimes give visiting children a pleasant activity to anticipate, too.

Stepmothers usually like having a stepchild bring a friend. The friend is likely to have fewer preconceived notions about her and can be easier for a stepmother to talk to. "It breaks the ice," maintained a stepmother who noticed that after her twelve-year-old stepdaughter's best friend announced that she liked her, her stepdaughter warmed to her more quickly.

Giving a child a room of his or her own is a nice idea, but unfortunately it's not always practical. There are other measures that can help make stepchildren feel familiar and that they belong in your home. A stepmother in whose house space was at a premium gave her stepchild a set of sheets printed with animal characters. "Though he always slept on the Hide-A-Bed, the sheets were his, something familiar," she reasoned. Older children might appreciate nightclothes, a special towel, a robe, or toilet articles—something of their own that stays behind.

TERMS

Regulating yourself and the conditions in your home during your stepchildren's visits is a gigantic part of coping with visitation, but it's not all. There may be some things that are outside your control.

There is usually a formal and legal basis to visitation, and its terms often annoy stepmothers, even those who get along beautifully with their stepchildren. Few women anticipate how restrictive—and inflexible—visitation agreements can be. One woman and her husband rose at 4:00 A.M. on Christmas Day in order to drive a hundred miles to pick up her stepchildren. Their mother wouldn't allow them to come on Christmas Eve: it wasn't written in the visitation agreement. Though the ex-wife's interpretation seems ridiculous to everyone except her and the judge who executed it, the stepmother and her husband were stuck with it despite several court appeals. Some things, absurd or not, can't be changed.

LONG-DISTANCE STEPMOTHERING

The length and frequency of a child's visits are the most important factors in determining how to handle visits. Obviously, if a stepchild lives far away and is spending his biannual weekend with you, then you shouldn't go out and leave him behind. On the other hand, if he's staying for several weeks, or comes every weekend, you can probably spend an evening out with a clear conscience. Coax a reluctant father by asking the child if he minds staying with a sitter or, in the case of older children, spending an evening with a book or a TV show. Sometimes those evenings are a welcome respite for children who are on center stage during too much of their visits. If the suitability of the sitter is a sticking point, perhaps a grandparent can be asked to help, or you can acquaint the child in advance with the sitter you have in mind. There are ways to get around the problem with initiative and preplanning.

The long-distance stepmother has different considerations.

Children who rarely visit usually get (and deserve) special treatment. When Martha's six-year-old stepson comes to visit his father for two weeks twice a year, his stay is considered a holiday. "He and my husband spend hours sitting in the middle of the river behind our house fishing. We always take him shopping for a new reel or waders," Martha said. She admitted that she and the other children in her household take a backseat when her stepson is around, but she doesn't begrudge him the attention he gets during his few visits. Stepchildren who visit more frequently are usually less disruptive.

The stepchild who lives far from his father often is a larger imposition for a stepmother than she expects. Normal life often comes to a halt when the child arrives. Visits must be planned to the letter, and commitments have to be made far in advance. When children visit infrequently, it's also much harder for a stepmother and stepchild to ease into an easy, familiar relationship. Developing trust and any kind of bond under these circumstances takes a long time and a lot of patience.

One of the ironic aspects of long-distance stepmothering is that a stepmother often ends up spending more time with her stepchildren during their visits than their father does. A stepmother of two preteen girls who live overseas with their mother found herself in charge of entertaining the girls for several weeks when their father's work suddenly demanded he travel to South America. "They didn't come to see me. They don't really like me much," stated their stepmother. But they spent two weeks together nonetheless.

When Amy's stepson's visitation period fell during the time that she and her husband were relocating to a new city, she had the full-time job of amusing six-year-old Sam while her husband worked long hours at his challenging new job. Amy, who had no experience with six-year-olds, was at a complete loss. Since she and her husband were unacquainted with the neighborhood, she was his only playmate day in and day out. Because of Sam, she was unable to concentrate on putting her new home in order. "I was an instant full-time mom. I felt that my husband stuck me with his responsibility," she remarked.

Her frustration turned to anger when her husband refused to leave Sam with a baby-sitter "in a strange place." As Amy said, "So that he could work *and* have Sam around, my wants were ignored. I was Sam's baby-sitter. Sam is a cute kid, but I dread his visits like the plague. I think they discharge my husband's obligations to Sam, but I'm not fooled for a minute when my husband says he loves being a parent. If he did, he'd manage to spend more time with him." Unsurprisingly, Amy has developed a closer relationship to Sam than his father has. "I'm the one who arranges for his day camp and leaves work early to pick him up when he's with us. I know him much better than his father does. I often resent caring for him, but I guess I feel sorry for him, too. I've decided to be there when I can be. I think he knows it."

There are some special techniques for handling these situations. A woman whose adolescent stepdaughters remained indifferent to her despite her attempts to be friendly, tired of taking them around town when they visited their father from Europe for two weeks, When she and her husband agreed to get them a hired companion to show them the sights in Washington, D.C., everyone was happier and more relaxed at dinnertime. The stepmother reported: "When they could get out on their own a little, away from me and the house, they relaxed, and so did I."

Stepchildren who visit infrequently pose other problems. The differences in standards of discipline, dress, and outlook are often glaring. Yet it's hardly worth a stepmother's time to lay down laws and try to make radical changes in their behavior. That approach is more likely to make the stepchildren feel they've landed in boot camp than to have any lasting effect. No one expects you to tolerate gross behavior, such as a child's sticking his gum under the dining table, but if a stepchild sleeps later than you believe is polite or healthy, let it pass (or perhaps play the piano or run the lawn mower). Sleeping until noon, habitual television viewing, junk-food eating, and poor dress are frequently heard complaints from stepmothers. One need not stock up on Twinkies for a junk-food junkie, but it simply doesn't pay to become angry every time a child puts a pretzel in his mouth.

One stepmother was furious to find wads of chocolate-bar wrappers and smeared candy in her stepdaughters' beds after they left. She obviously couldn't keep them from eating candy, but she did stop making up their beds with floral designer sheets. While the episode took much of the fun out of preparing for their visits, accepting the reality of the girls' habits decreased her anger. Similarly, if a stepchild habitually arrives with unsuitable clothes, anticipate it next time. Make an advance birthday or Christmas present of a nice jacket or dress and suggest that it be worn to an occasion you plan to attend with the child during his or her visit. There's a certain virtue to accepting what you cannot change and working around it.

The stepmothering experience is as inconstant as all human nature, and maybe a little more so. Some days are clearly better than others. "Mostly, I like my stepdaughter," a typical stepmother said. "Five percent of the time I don't like her. Another five percent of the time I don't want her around, which may or may not have anything to do with how I feel about her." There's probably not a stepmother alive whose enthusiasm for her stepchildren's visits doesn't wane occasionally. Sometimes it may have to do with the kids, sometimes with her. Just about the time you think you've got visitation licked, something changes. The stepdaughter you felt so sanguine about last month drops out of college and takes up with a loathsome fellow. Next fall she may be back at school, a pleasure to have around. But *you* may be in a slump, swamped with obligations and feeling antisocial, not much like having an energetic coed around. Such changes are the reality of stepmothering, and visitation brings this reality home.

10

Discipline

iscipline stumps most stepmothers. The ambiguous nature of our relations to our stepchildren—and our authority over them—causes a great deal of uncertainty. At the very least, we should have the authority to control the way our stepchildren behave in our own household. Almost all stepmothers would agree, but when asked how to exert that control, most of us start shuffling our feet and looking for an exit. We don't know.

Custodial stepmoms have difficulty deciding how to go about setting and enforcing limits, but at least their right to discipline is usually undisputed. Noncustodial stepmothers are invariably less certain. And to complicate matters further, both groups want to be liked, so both often lack disciplinary conviction.

The uncertain status of a stepchild in your home is the primary cause of this dilemma. Stepchildren are a special brand of visitor, related to one member of your home. Most children don't act like guests either, and they shouldn't be treated as such if you're aiming for easy, genial times together.

The question is, how should a stepmother expect them to behave? Should they act like family or like model guests? Should they treat her home as their home, or even as a special haven, someplace where they don't have to hang up their clothes? Prevailing wisdom says they should approach it as their home—a place to feel comfortable and entitled—but *at* your home—a place to be respectful of the atmosphere and rules. The stepmother must bend to grant her stepchild the former, and the child must comply with the second. The trade sounds easier than it is for most stepfamilies.

Stepmothers who live with their stepchildren might differ, but noncustodial stepmothers generally feel that the special conditions surrounding visitation are more difficult to adjust to than having stepchildren full-time. The sporadic nature of visits is definitely a handicap. Relationships develop slowly. Problems take longer to work out. "At least if they lived here, I would be the boss. Our roles would be clear. Now we're neither fish nor fowl," said a stepmother, weary of feeling suspended between intermittent visits, of constantly putting her efforts and these new relationships on hold.

The fuzzy nature of your authority over your stepchildren makes them feel strange about taking orders from you, too. Family counselors advise couples to come out and say that it's a difficult, tense time for everyone. You may need to question the reasons for unruly behavior before you judge a child too harshly. One stepmother used the analogy of crossing a river. She told her stepson, who demonstrated his anger and anxiety by always throwing his coat on the floor rather than hanging it up, that the period they were all going through was like being in a boat and trying to get to the other side. "It's important that kids feel you're all in this together. You can admit it's tough," states a psychologist who approves of a straightforward approach to relieve tension.

Professionals warn against excessive discipline. It frustrates your stepchildren and stunts the development of personal relationships. "Take a backseat for a long time," suggests Dr. Clifford Sager. "Strive to be an appropriate adult friend instead of a disciplinarian." But don't be a pushover either.

The practical application of this middle ground is hard to achieve. Emily Visher gave a good example of a gentle disciplining technique that parents may be more familiar with than stepmothers. "Don't tell a child, 'Stop biting your nails.' Instead say, 'I can see that you bite your nails. Would you like me to help you try to break the habit?'" The second approach, without putting a child as much on the defensive, registers your complaint and opinion. A stepmother is usually more comfortable with this less aggressive manner.

It's important for your stepchildren to see that you and your husband share the authority to discipline. You must be perceived as one of the chiefs, not just another Indian. Emily and John Visher advise, "While discipline is not usually accepted by stepchildren until a friendly relationship has been established (often a matter of eighteen to twenty-four months), both adults do need to support each other's authority in the household. The natural parent may be the primary disciplinarian initially, but when that person is unavailable, it is often necessary for that parent to give a clear message to the children that the stepparent is acting as an authority figure in his or her absence."

Stepmothers fear discipline, and for good reason. Natural parents nurture their children with love and care before they set limits for them. Under those circumstances most children find discipline easier to take. A stepmother needs to demonstrate that she cares for a child before she can be truly effective as an authority figure. "I think if I'd asked my stepdaughter to do anything when we first moved in together, she would have deeply resented it. So I always took her dad aside and told him to tell her. Then I'd strongly second his suggestion to her. But now that we've been together for three years, I've earned the right to have my say. I do her laundry, fix her meals, and shop for her matching T-shirts. So it's okay for me to tell her a thing or two for her own good," reported a stepmother.

As every parent knows, kids take advantage of the presence of a stranger or newcomer because they think they can get away with more. They also sense insecurity in their parent. "I told my husband, 'You're terrorized by your children.' He tried to *talk* his eight-year-old daughter out of misbehaving—doing things like filling the tub with too much water. When she ignored him, he just walked away," Margo said. "I was taken by surprise by this kind of nitty-gritty parenting when my husband's kids started to visit. I didn't think I'd need to get involved. *Ha!*"

Margo finally intervened in one dispute between her stepdaughter, April, and her father when April ignored her father's command to pick up her shoes. When her father started to do it for her, Margo stopped him. Then she gave the order to April, who began to see that her stepmother wasn't going to be a pushover. April decided to pick up her shoes.

Most bad habits are those that went uncorrected at the beginning of steprelationships. Restraint and understanding are always advised, but you don't have to give in to unreasonable demands. A woman who allowed her stepson to be excused during dinner to telephone his mother regrets not asking him to wait until after dinner now that his midmeal phone call has become a ritual. "If I go back on it now, it seems as if I'm trying to be mean," she said. Of course, she and her husband should run that risk; they should have done so sooner.

Whenever another woman's stepchildren visited, they insisted on sitting in the front seat of the car with their father while she sat in the back. Her husband acquiesced. "It made me furious with them all. They didn't have the right to relegate me," she stated. Finally, she reestablished her position. "I told them, sorry, I was going to sit in the front seat, and that was it. I felt a lot better, and it didn't hurt them to sit in back." When rules are given with conviction, they are less likely to be disputed.

CUSTODIAL STEPMOTHERING

Professionals single out discipline as the biggest obstacle for custodial stepmothers. You may more easily learn to live with a man who refuses to hang up his clothes or smokes in bed than you can sit by and watch behavior of which you disapprove. "My husband spoiled his daughter. It was obvious to me that I was going to be regarded as the mean stepmother even when I set down the most basic rules. Yet he wasn't around the house, so all the household duties and discipline shifted to me. I was the one who had to dish out the commands my stepdaughter would like least—to clean her room, do the dishes, and so on," a stepmother said. She and her husband agreed when they married that he would discipline his nine-year-old daughter. "We thought she'd like me better if he was the one who cracked down on her. I was to be a 'supervisory' figure and leave the discipline to him. The whole plan was ridiculous. He felt protective of her, and I lacked the confidence to tell her what to do. When he came home, I itemized her shortcomings, which made me seem like a shrew. She knew my word didn't stick. We just weren't realistic."

Another woman who tried a similar approach reported that her husband's arrival each evening became hilarious. "His two kids and I raced each other out to the garage to see who could start in first with their version of an argument." Obviously, this is not the way to run a stepfamily. A stepmother must be brave, and her husband must support her.

A UNITED FRONT

A couple should agree on discipline. Partners should talk it over privately to arrive at some shared approach. They may want to revise and review strategy as time goes on, but discipline will always be a major issue. Children are geniuses at playing one adult against the other if they know they're at odds, so a united front is essential, especially with such strong-willed creatures as adolescents.

Early discussion of rules and limits for a child can prevent many misunderstandings between marriage partners, and it also demonstrates your willingness to be involved. Both of you get the chance to reexamine your theories and possibly formulate new ones. Because so many of our attitudes about proper behavior stem from our own upbringing, they are often buried in our subconscious. One woman was amazed to discover how strongly she felt about curfews when her teenage stepdaughter visited her and her husband on the military post where they lived. "My husband went to bed while I waited up for her. I sounded like my own mother, but I believed there was a decent hour for her to get home. Maybe I was a little bit conservative, but my husband got the message that I really did care for Patty. I think he was surprised that I could be such a mother hen."

Another stepmother found her husband's disciplinary techniques too harsh to suit her. "He would lash out at his children, and though I disagreed, I didn't interfere. I felt I didn't have a right," she reported. When she finally broached the topic, she discovered that he felt overburdened as the sole disciplinarian and readily welcomed her help. Together they settled on a disciplinary approach that involved her and included more of her values and approaches. "Before, I felt like a baby-sitter, on the outside looking in," she said.

The age of the children and their emotional well-being obviously require consideration and sensitivity on a stepmother's part. Wisely, she may choose to suspend her authority to discipline during a rough settling-in period, but eventually, according to counselor Thomas Seibt, "They've got to know who's boss, that you have the authority when you decide to use it, and that you are not their peer."

Discipline issues usually expose your opinion of your stepchildren to your husband, and that, too, can be a delicate matter. Biological parents are not truly expected to see their children objectively. A stepmother often has a more objective vantage point, but her husband may tend to dismiss her critical observations as prejudice. Natural parents also feel defensive and protective of their children against outsiders, and at least initially, the stepmother is an outsider.

Discipline cannot be used as a method to mold stepchildren into what you would like them to be. On the contrary, step-mothers usually feel that their authority gets low priority. "What I want from my stepchildren is always second to what their parents want. My authority counts less. My idea of what's good for them never gets first consideration," noted one woman. Hers is a common complaint. A stepmother must content herself with controlling the behavior and issues that affect her, her family affairs, and their times together. For you, discipline is a way to control conditions in your home and when you are together. It is usually not the way to make a long-term imprint on a stepchild's behavior or personality.

The prevailing opinion among stepmothers is that stepchildren are spoiled, and in many respects, family psychologists agree. Biological parents typically make excuses for them because of their own guilt associated with the trauma of divorce. In cases where a youngster can take refuge from one parent's authority by running to the other parent, a child of divorce can avoid discipline and corrective measures almost indefinitely. Bad behavior proliferates. But it's a loaded topic for the stepmother, who is well advised to save harsh criticism until she has established with her husband a record of having her stepchild's best interests in mind. It takes patience and strategy, but it can be worthwhile.

In matters of discipline, you have to earn your own way with your husband, too. Marilyn got nowhere with her husband when she pointed out that his daughter, eight-year-old Allison, who constantly interrupted her elders and took to her bed when things didn't go her way, needed discipline. Some extra effort helped Marilyn earn her husband's confidence. "At first I let Tom do all the caring for Allison. He was good at it, and it kept me free, but it also meant we lived in two camps: Tom and I and Tom and Allison," she said. So Marilyn became the one to hold Allison's head when she vomited after her birthday party. She hemmed Allison's band uniform the night before the school parade. She also found teachers at Allison's school who told her that Allison was always complaining in class and pouted if she wasn't the first to be called upon. When Marilyn reported back to Tom, he no longer responded with "Let up on Allison."

THE INDIRECT APPROACH

When a stepmother can't discipline a stepchild directly—or fears a backlash from her husband if she does—relatives can help her to register criticism with her husband. One father refused to agree with his second wife that his son's table manners needed improvement until the boy's aunt, at the stepmother's request, broached the subject with him. Nobody ever said stepmothering simplified life. In this minefield of human relations, it sometimes takes three grown-ups to tell one boy how to use a fork properly.

11

Housekeeping

Even women who seldom set foot in their own kitchen, scorn housework, and don't concern themselves with ring around the collar find that having kids around makes housekeeping an issue. Your domestic style and standards confront theirs. Subconsciously, at least, your home is your territory, and the way it is maintained and treated is surprisingly important to you. But talking about it gives many stepmothers the shivers.

Asking stepchildren to tidy up after themselves in the bathroom, certainly a reasonable request, causes a stepmother to worry that they will dislike her, that she is unkind, or that she is failing her husband. Her desire to be liked, coupled with a nagging uncertainty about her authority over her stepchildren, can sabotage her attempts at discipline. She can't very well tell them to change their ethics or their lives if she disapproves of them, but she can oversee their accommodations and assert some household rules, much as a schoolteacher or camp counselor might. At this point hers is usually a crisis of confidence.

A stepmother of two teenage sons who visit her home weekly reported she was a nervous wreck after their first few visits. The boys expected dinner to be set before them and cleared away. The stepmother, who waited on them, soon began to feel like their maid. On Sunday nights after they left, she angrily stewed over what she considered to be their bad manners and lack of consideration—and complained to her husband about it.

Her enthusiasm for the boys' weekly visits plummeted, but then she took charge. Finally, she announced at a family dinner: "We don't have a housekeeper here, and I expect you to take your dishes to the sink. I'd even like you to help make dinner next week." The boys exchanged surprised glances across the table, but they did what was asked, and a new routine was established. They'll never know that she rehearsed her speech to them in front of the bathroom mirror several times before she composed herself enough to make it.

When Suzie married a man with two sons five years ago, she hurled herself enthusiastically into stepmothering. "I tackled it like a career," she asserted. She took orders for their favorite foods before they came. She and her husband organized outings, such as trips to Red Sox games, before most visits. "I couldn't believe it when the youngest boy picked at his food and said he didn't like the mushrooms in my steak sauce. He wouldn't eat it. It was so rude. We were all sitting around the table, and I was on the verge of tears." When the boys didn't clean up after themselves, make their beds, or hang up their soggy towels, she was furious—but silent. "On Saturdays I just kept telling myself, 'Sunday will come soon. Just twenty-four hours to go.'" Hoping for Sunday to come is how too many stepmothers spend their time. It can become a tedious and destructive weekend syndrome.

Suzie's grin-and-bear-it approach became the root of many dissatisfactions with her role. All week she rationalized that she shouldn't say anything about how miserable she felt on weekends, and all weekend she waited for Sunday. Four years later, after a year of therapy and marriage counseling related directly to stepmothering, she gives some strong advice: "Exercise your role as an adult and a parent right away. You are not their peer. Tell them what you want. Otherwise, you've had it. They don't hate real parents for telling them what to do, and they won't hate you either. But if you don't do it, you'll end up hating yourself."

Nobody suggests that a stepmother should come on like Stepmommie Dearest, but she should stand up for the way she expects things to be done in her home and her right to say so. This is probably her toughest job: handling herself, preserving her integrity, and asserting her natural right to be there. Her style depends on her personality and her stepchildren, of course. Obviously, if you come on strong to kids who are timid and doelike, you may wish that you'd tempered your tone. One self-described "direct Jewish mother-type" said she had difficulty learning how to understand and talk with stepchildren who, in her opinion, communicate in "inaudible squeaks." It can take a while to crack their code.

Regardless of how foreign your stepchildren's tongue seems to you, speak directly to them, not through your husband. You can't expect kids to trust you if you're a pussycat in person and then they learn through their father that you rage like a lion behind closed doors.

Most of us learn the hard way. One stepmother tried to be perfect and loving around her stepsons. They tracked dirt on her floors, raided the refrigerator, and showed up late for dinner, but she looked on beatifically and said nothing. But after her husband and the boys left the house in the morning, she called her husband's office. The 10:00 A.M. phone call to her husband became routine. "I told him everything I wanted him to tell the boys. I'd start right in: 'Tell Rob to hang up his towels, tell Jeff to take out the garbage, and that the next time he's coming home for dinner to call by six or else.' I could be real tough with my husband. I just couldn't say it to the boys," she stated. She was taken aback one evening when her husband wearily walked in the door and told his sons, while she looked on, "Your step-mother called today and told me to tell you guys…" She said, "I felt like such a fool. Jeff and Rob looked at me like I was the biggest coward they'd ever seen. I was livid at my husband, but I could see he was right. I'd done it to myself. From that day forward I told them myself what I wanted them to do. It wasn't so hard, and I ended up feeling a lot better."

Stepmothers often complain about being caught in the homemaker/maid syndrome. Catering to stepchildren with whom they have no prior relationship feels unnatural, some-times even a little like abuse. A stepmother's contribution seems out of proportion to her genuine involvement with the stepchil-dren. Psychologists, who repeatedly hear women moan and groan about this predicament, advise, "Don't do it." Nobody says that a stepmother has to assume all the homemaking and hostessing (read, *motherly*) chores for her stepchildren, especially if she resents doing them. Most husbands, when alerted to their wife's negative feelings about such tasks, would rather pitch in and help with meals and accommodations than have the burden create bitter feelings. In fact, fathers may welcome the opportunity to nurture and work closely with their children at the household chores that visiting children generate. They may enjoy marketing, cooking, or setting a table together, and a stepmother can give them a nudge in that direction.

Furthermore, visiting stepchildren usually appreciate the chance to work on something constructive in their parent's new home. It makes them feel that they belong, unlike the special trips and outings, which tend to emphasize their outsider status. A stepmother who resents being responsible for meals and other chores may feel more relaxed working alongside her husband and children in a joint project. She's also less likely to feel like an outsider.

Stepmothers who work usually have more trouble adjusting to visitation than nonworking women do because working women resent filling what little spare time they have with children and chores. Though many natural mothers work, they have practice juggling the routines and strains that children pose, but part-time stepmothers don't. "I get resentful," admitted a stepmother who wishes her husband would come home early and help with the meals when his children are in town. "I have to remind him that I'm thirty-seven years old and I've been childless all my life until now. He can't expect me to be a perfect parent overnight. He's got to help." Again, there is no substitute for working together.

Household rules and standards for behavior invariably add to a stepmother's general confusion and frustration. It's fine to be flexible and accommodating to stepchildren, but don't let them take over or change the way you do things. They *can* adapt to your practices and housekeeping style the same way they adapt to rules at school and at their friends' homes. But you have to tell them what you expect of them. They can't read your mind. It's perfectly all right to say, "Here we do it this way," or "I wish you would do such and such." In fact, family counselors suggest a stepmother use those lines to counter the children's assertions that "at home we do it like this."

Taking charge is a self-protective and healthy practice for stepmothers despite their reluctance. Women who don't assert some authority over their stepchildren invariably feel resentful—and about as effective as a new baby-sitter or substitute teacher feels. Their stepchildren begin to seem like invaders. It's not fair either to you or to the children if you allow your dread to develop to the point that you can't muster the courage to perform as a grown-up. If you want to be in charge, take charge. When it comes to housekeeping, stepmothering means being the boss.

12

Married Life

S tepchildren can strain even the best of marriages. Women inexperienced with children
may be slow to recognize this truth, but we
soon learn otherwise. Even visiting stepchildren
saddle a marriage with many of the issues and
responsibilities of parenting.

One woman said, "I was envious of my
husband's ex-wife. She had her weekends free,
but I had the typical parent hassles: no privacy
and not enough time." Another grumbled, "The
kids dictate our social life as a couple. Now we
spend most of our time with other parents on
weekends. I miss seeing our old friends, who are
mostly people without children."

Because the majority of stepmothers are noncustodial, combining leisure activities that refresh and renew a couple with the
presence of children is an important task for marriage partners.
Since stepchildren typically visit on weekends, adult pastimes
and family activities inevitably conflict. Too much of either one
usually catches up with husband and wife.

Most remarried couples, at least the stepmother half, don't
want to stay home the entire time that their stepchildren are visiting. Sometimes fathers do. They are reluctant to leave their
children with a baby-sitter and feel obliged to focus their atten
tion on their children. The stepmother of a six-year-old who
visits her home regularly takes a strong position: "Kids are kids
and adults are adults, and kids shouldn't go every place adults
go." She refuses to take her stepdaughter along to parties with
her adult friends, but her husband wants his daughter with them.
So everybody stays home, and everyone is unhappy.

These differences are bound to affect the balance of a marital
relationship. Whether stepchildren are custodial or not, a husband and wife must work at controlling the demands that children make on them. Children shouldn't be treated as enemies,
but partners need to recognize that when left uncontrolled,
stepchildren can detract from and even threaten some marriages.

A husband and wife can cope with only a given number
of external considerations and still move ahead in their own
relationship. For most remarried couples with stepchildren
it requires constant effort to prevent the issues surrounding
stepchildren from dominating them or at least demanding a disproportionate share of their time and attention. Sometimes those
considerations undermine a marriage indirectly by affecting
how partners interact when conflicts regarding stepchildren
prevail.

You must learn to be conscious of their effect on you and your marriage as a consequence. Refusing to recognize them and sublimating your aggravations and real feelings doesn't work. The effect on you alone is generally enough to distort your personality and to disturb the balance in a marriage.

"It was so hard on me when the children came that I just put up a wall between me and my husband and his kids," one stepmother recalled. "I know it sounds crazy, but I just wanted them to come and get it over with. When they went home, I could forget them." She also became hypercritical of the children after they'd gone home. "Of course, I always coated my criticism with concern, but I needed to point out all their faults to my husband." Not surprisingly, this woman found that she and her husband eventually barely discussed his children. "They were his, not mine," she said.

Her cold and overly self-protective approach created a gulf between them. It also backfired. In the end, it was she who was alienated in the stepfamily. The children and their father maintained a continuing relationship while she remained stranded alone—the stereotype of a wicked stepmother. Happy endings in stepfamilies always require openness and involvement. Emotionally isolating yourself from your husband is the worst condition that can happen to marriages.

Partners in these marriages desperately need to confide in each other, to share their points of view, and to become aware of each other's positions. If they can begin before marriage, so much the better, but unfortunately few couples do. As a result, stepmothers often feel locked in to a situation that they would like to adapt and modify, but they feel guilty. And when they are ready to act, they fear it may be too late.

MOTIVES

Let's be honest. We take on stepchildren in order to have good marriages. We clearly cannot prosper in marriage without becoming involved with our stepchildren. We don't want to be left out of this important area of our husband's life. One step-mother admitted she was cool to her stepchildren at first. While she and her husband were dating, she even preferred that he visit his children without her. "They weren't a reality to me then," she said. But as their relationship showed signs of permanence, she recalled, "I felt jealous of these unknown, faceless figures. I finally took an interest because I didn't want to be excluded. I wanted them to include me."

A sense of urgency usually accompanies this sentiment. Once the reality of having joined a family soaks in, a stepmother typically feels that she must be accepted by her stepchildren in order to advance in the family *and* in her marriage. Visits can become pass-or-fail exams for her. However, stepchildren don't always respond that way. They won't budge under pressure, so your family life becomes divided into your marriage on the one hand and your relationship with your stepchildren on the other, each developing at a different rate. The division can spoil your hopes for an idealized whole, especially when notions about that big happy family are still lurking around.

SOME NICE THINGS

Stepchildren don't have to be detrimental to a marriage. If you are flexible enough to accept the unexpected, your stepchildren may have a positive effect on you and your husband. Sometimes they provide a nice bonus by drawing the two of you together, in much the same way that natural children can convert a couple into a family.

Young children, responsive to care and attention, often generate a cozy family atmosphere. "The children drew us closer, which I never expected," stated the forty-year-old stepmother of a four- and a nine-year-old. " To my total surprise, a family feeling took us over. We carried it with us when we took the kids to visit friends or relatives, or wherever we went." She and her husband even added some family practices to their lifestyle. They went to church on Sundays and began making regular trips to amusement parks. "I can't explain it, but we got a glow from it. It was a new feeling," she said.

It's heartening to note that this was said by a stepmother who at the start of her marriage wanted to pull her hair out over a rigid, "ridiculous" visitation schedule. Her example shows that one set of problems need not determine your stepmothering experience. No stepmothering situation will be flawless, but it's the final balance that matters.

FAMILY VERSUS MARRIAGE

The stepfamily version of a "big happy family"—even when it exists—has some drawbacks. A marriage can suffer at the expense of the "happy gang." With numerous personalities and relationships to keep track of, adult relationships often become obscured by parenting concerns. As Jane found out, "Too much of the time the children's concerns overshadowed our relationship. The community became the most important thing. My husband and I were absorbed with shopping for shoes, with parent-teacher conferences, and with doctors' appointments. There was no peace or tranquillity when the children were little. I don't think I could have stood it if my husband wasn't a romantic person. Fortunately, we made the most of our time alone, but it was a tough test," she said. Her experience at combining four children with five stepchildren is proof that the his-and-hers stepfamily mix can succeed, but only because they stayed flexible.

This marriage suffered its worst strains over issues of discipline. "My husband was more relaxed about curfews and some drug experimentation than I was. I couldn't stand his attitude," she reported. At a low point, she threw a pan of eggs at him during a squabble about the rules for a slumber party in their basement.

TALKING THINGS OVER

Repeated advice to hash things over makes remarriage with stepchildren sound like one endless encounter session, but communication is an essential ingredient of successful remarriages with stepchildren. The ability to discuss your hopes and complaints frankly with each other is a necessity—not an option. Patterns of estrangement, of keeping your own counsel, of allowing matters to fester, and of other unconstructive attitudes are hard to break.

A stepmother of four said that for thirty years, "my husband and I never discussed how difficult I found being a stepmother. He couldn't tolerate hearing a word against his children, so I kept my resentments to myself. It could have been so much easier if we had talked. The one thing I would tell somebody marrying a divorced man with kids today is to start talking about what is going on with the children and how you feel about it at once. Otherwise it *will* affect your marriage."

Sometimes it takes a while to feel comfortable about criticizing, complaining, or just plain sounding off about matters pertaining to your stepchildren, but once you feel secure enough with your husband, speaking your mind becomes easier. It is never advisable to criticize your husband's children gratuitously. He is going to react defensively if you call them names or threaten to bar them from your household. But loving partners should be able to talk about their feelings—even when what they have to say isn't all happy talk.

"When I first began living with my husband, I wouldn't say a word about his kids or tell him what I really wanted from him and from them. But now that we have more history together, I know he's not going to leave me or shut me out because I'm furious with his kids for a day," a stepmother stated. It would be unnatural for a stepmother not to have some feelings and opinions about her stepchildren that differ from her husband's.

Astonishingly few stepmothers say that they discussed visitation with their husband-to-be before they were married, and virtually all of them were surprised with the situation that evolved later. "I was so starry-eyed and in love, I never thought to ask my husband what he had in mind for a visitation schedule," said a stepmother who was taken aback when her stepchildren came every weekend. They hadn't visited their father nearly so often when she was dating him. "It is just amazing how many couples avoid this important subject," observes Clifford Sager.

No amount of discomfort over broaching the subject before marriage can compare to the anguish that disagreements about visitation cause later. Melanie's husband took his three children away to the seaside and left her alone—without their car—in the city nearly every weekend after their wedding. "We fought about it every time. I was miserable," she said, and thirteen years later she is still resentful of that period. "If we had only talked about it beforehand, we would have been cooler and more careful," she reflected. In her opinion the arrangement threatened their marriage, and she believes it was saved only because her husband was transferred overseas. There, without the problem of weekly visitation, he and she were able to strengthen their marriage as they had not been able to before. When they returned to the United States, her husband was more comfortable bringing his wife and children together. "We needed to be a couple first, and I'm not sure we could have established that with the visitation issue between us the way it was before we left. Our marriage might not have survived," Melanie stated.

Most couples don't have a transfer to rescue them from visitation troubles. Professionals strongly urge remarried partners to discuss visitation plans before marriage or, if that is not possible, at least to discuss the repercussions on their relationship at the first sign of strain. Wounds and resentments over differences can and do prevent a couple from building a solid marriage foundation, and they can indeed threaten a marriage.

"It's never smart to wait and hope for the best," concludes Dr. Sager. Early in a marriage it might be wise for a stepmother to go along with a visitation plan or two, even if she is doubtful about them, in order to demonstrate her good intentions and flexibility. But if the arrangements are seriously troubling, as they were for Melanie, it is better to proclaim a crisis than to wait for one to be inflicted on you. Professionals say that stepmothers must share responsibility for the relationships and living conditions that evolve in a stepfamily. Acquiescing to an undesirable situation makes you one of the guilty parties.

Becoming aware of each other's true feelings is sometimes difficult for husbands and wives who love each other. Good intentions often inhibit the kind of open conversation that couples need most. New marriage partners, full of enthusiasm and goodwill, mistakenly try to conceal their anxieties, but this tendency works against them if it obscures their willingness to recognize complex problems and work together toward solutions. In critical situations, dominated by high emotions and heated disagreements, professional advice can usually help.

Can your husband truly be a soulmate and best friend to you when you have a problem that is indirectly his fault? The answer is yes, if your motives toward him are caring and friendly, too. Don't think of yourself as a victim and him as the perpetrator of your ills. If you establish yourselves as a team that works together not only to plan the schedules and events of your life but also to work and sustain a close married relationship, you can succeed.

13

Vacations

A vacation is a time to get away from work and the everyday world, but a family vacation can be quite a different animal. And a family vacation with stepchildren is the strangest animal of all.

One stepmother reported: "When we went on vacation with Terry's kids, we always ate in cafeterias or fast-food restaurants. I thought we'd get one elegant dinner together, linger over coffee, have a nightcap, take a walk after dinner, but no way. Terry wanted to spend all his time with his kids to make up for the rest of the year. I won't get more time off until next year, and believe me, I'm not going to spend it like that again."

Vacation and holiday planning invariably strains stepfamilies. In modern busy lives, time away becomes precious to married couples. A stepmother (and most other people, for that matter) tends to think of a vacation as a right rather than a bonus. If stepchildren figure into every vacation, she may begin to feel cheated. "When Jack says he's got two weeks of vacation coming this summer I feel myself tighten up," said Rosemary, a stepmother to three children. "If we do what seems right by the children, Jack and I have no time alone away from our full schedules. It's my vacation time, too, and I don't want to spend all of it caring for kids."

Children who live apart from their fathers think that they, too, have a right to Daddy when he isn't working, and they're right. The conflict is obvious. The man in the middle may try to satisfy both sides at once without realizing that it can't usually be done. "We can afford only one trip yearly, and we always go across country to see my stepson," Miriam stated. By itself, she said, that wouldn't be so bad, except that in order to cut costs, she and her husband stay with her parents, who live near her stepson's home. "My stepson comes to stay with us at their home, so there I am on vacation with my stepson at my parents' house. There's cooking, housework, and all the demands from both sides. I don't call that a vacation. I dread it." Both spouses have the right to enjoy their money and spare time, but saying it doesn't make it so. How does a remarried couple go about it? The solution lies in planning and joint decision making.

"A husband has to appreciate that the spouse would like time alone," states Clifford Sager, adding that the desire for time alone is no different in stepfamilies than in biological families. "Everyone needs a respite," he asserts, but in remarried families there's a greater potential for guilt and competition among family members. So vacation plans and commitments should not be made haphazardly—or unilaterally. A husband and wife need to put their wants out on the table and to construct a vacation scheme from there. The task is nearly a stepfamily art form.

While financial circumstances, personalities, available time, and many other personal factors must be taken into account, there's one cardinal rule for everybody: anticipate. "We don't promise the boys anything until we've talked everything over ourselves," reported a stepmother who was once reluctant to speak up when she wanted time away from her stepsons. "Whenever we came back from vacation, I was mad for weeks, feeling cheated and mournful that our chance for time together was past." Her husband used to promise to spend his entire summer vacation with his sons, but now he waits until he and his wife have agreed on dates that allow for a few days alone before or after the boys are invited to join them. In much the same way that the myth of one big happy family must be dispelled for stepfamilies, the family-vacation scenario in which everyone is jammed together for two weeks with a shaggy dog in the station wagon is also obsolete—if everybody wants to stay sane and a couple wants to stay married. Custom-made schedules that allow for private time in addition to family time may require only minimal adjustments, yet they can do a world of good toward helping stepmothers feel that they are still wives as well as stepmothers—and making a vacation a success rather than a disaster.

Planning requires honesty from both partners, but vacations seem to be an area in which guilt and romantic expectations often inhibit frankness. The father feels guilty for having too little time with his children year-round. His wife feels guilty that she doesn't want her stepchildren along. She may anticipate spontaneous romance and prefer not to try to legislate it.

A remarried couple will have to learn to juggle the demands of the family and the needs of the twosome. The couple that neglects its own need for privacy is foolish. Recent surveys consider lack of time together as the chief enemy of happy marriages. Remarried partners, who have an abundance of extra demands on their time, must be even more vigilant in their efforts to get enough time together. Family experts Fredrick Capaldi and Barbara McRae, in their book *Stepfamilies: A Cooperative Responsibility*, suggest that partners in a second marriage with stepchildren get away alone together for a weekend at least every six weeks in order to escape the extra strains of the remarried family and to focus on each other.

A stepmother who wants time alone with her husband shouldn't feel guilt. The benefits can be appreciable, especially if they renew her willingness to join in family vacations, affirm her identity as a marriage partner, and help minimize the threatening aspect of stepchildren for her. Natural parents expect children to respect their need for such time. Remarried parents should expect the same.

Of course, the way you approach your husband on the subject is important. Don't begin by attacking your stepchildren or opposing his need to be with them. Stress the positive things about getting away together instead. "Give him the message that you would love to be alone with him, that you adore him," advises Emily Visher. Stress a positive desire. Saying that you don't want to be with the kids puts the emphasis in the wrong place.

Vacations cause controversy mostly because they are so rare. "We obviously can't afford two king-size vacations," said a stepmother of two young children, so she and her husband alternate the kind of vacation they take. Last year they went on the "king-size" trip to Florida for a week with his children. Then they spent another week home together without them, making home repairs and going to movies. This year they will use the king-size vacation budget to go to a resort alone. The week with the children will be spent at home or on day trips to nearby recreation sites. "Maybe this year we'll have a cookout for their friends or join the local swim club," the stepmother said.

My husband and I set some similar rules for ourselves. Some vacations are reserved for ourselves. Another, a winter ski trip, was declared a family affair from the outset so that there would be no confusion (chiefly in my mind) that it was intended to be a private retreat. We kept a day or two for ourselves after my stepdaughters left. It seemed to work well that time, chiefly, I believe, because we planned it that way.

The stepmother who does not have her own children is at a special disadvantage when it comes to vacation and holiday planning. If this is her first marriage, the demands that her stepchildren make on these occasions are especially distressing because of her typically high romantic expectations for leisure time. Clifford Sager and the coauthors of the professional guidebook *Treating the Remarried Family* explain: "This spouse may expect exclusivity and romance in the relationships, while the divorced spouse may expect solidity, security, and full family life."

These differences, dormant much of the time, come to life over vacations. Some stepmothers react fiercely to plans that offer them no escape from family roles and children. A small issue like taking the kids to Yellowstone for a week can become a big deal for remarried partners who don't take some of these emotional issues into account.

The vacation that is intended to be all things to all people is bound to fail. A trip that is designed to be restful, romantic, and recuperative for a couple, fun and educational for kids, unifying for parent and child, and beneficial for a stepmother and stepchild is doomed to be a disappointment.

The expectations heaped onto one family's month-long vacation every summer eventually became more than the parents or children could bear. "We dutifully trooped off together on a big month-long family vacation every year for five years," recalled the stepmother. "We all felt obligated to be on our best behavior. I bent over backward to be as hospitable and as motherly as possible to my husband's children. Everyone was polite, but nobody relaxed. By the end of it I was saying—between sobs— that it was not fun, that this was my only vacation and I wasn't enjoying it. The kids were sullen and slamming doors at us. But we vowed to do it again every year. It was a challenge, as though if we just worked harder at it we'd get the hang of it."

They never did get the hang of it, and when a psychologist who was treating her stepson suggested that it might be constructive for the family to forgo their annual month-long family vacation, the stepmother said, "It was a great relief for everyone. We stopped trying to pretend that we had something together that we really didn't have."

All stepfamily vacations are not doomed, but they shouldn't be required when relationships and personalities don't lend themselves to the project. Once the need for private time has been met, a family vacation can have advantages. For instance, on a trip, a noncustodial stepmother is generally relieved of her household role, so she and her stepchildren may find themselves relaxing and discovering a new environment together. Just looking out for the right motel or restaurant can be a shared experience. With more time to spare, time becomes less precious. A father and child can spend an afternoon together, and there's still time left over for the family or the couple.

Relations become less intense. A stepmother and stepchild begin to accumulate a history of their own. "The time we went to Nashville" or "the time we were stranded in Evanston" become precious memories in these expanding relationships. There's also time to have a disagreement, to make up, to bounce back, to be yourselves.

A new stepmother of a five- and an eight-year-old was pleasantly surprised by the effect on their relationship of a two-week car trip. "We quit tiptoeing around each other. We *had* to be involved together. All the adjustments had to be made." When her stepdaughter threw a tantrum in the backseat of their car, both her father and his wife took her in hand. "She gave me some cockamamie excuse for acting like that, and I swore at her. She looked a little shocked. I meant business and she knew it. We'd suddenly come light-years. I'd probably never have said that at home."

"We made a lot of progress as a family," she said. Being on the road together requires teamwork. "Somebody gasses up the car, somebody takes the kids to the bathroom. You're all less self-conscious and freer." Her positive feelings about family vacations grew when she and her husband concluded that despite the success of their family trip, it did not substitute for time alone. "It made us conscious of the time we do need alone, so we're planning a vacation just for ourselves in the fall." Furthermore, her husband, who used to feel guilty about taking a vacation without his children, felt absolved. "He did his duty. We all had fun. He won't feel guilty leaving them next time," she stated.

Some stepchildren do not lend themselves to relaxation under even the best vacation circumstances. "We went to the beach, and Michael was unhappy. We went skiing and Michael was cold. We stayed home and Michael hated the city. Trying to please Michael takes over wherever we go," said a stepmother who has repeatedly tried to have a successful trip with her husband's only son. Her husband feels obliged to take the boy, who lives in another state, but she is beginning to reconsider. "I think Michael and his father should go away together, try to work some things out."

She may be right. A psychologist related the story of a troubled eight-year-old girl who was unhappy and a considerable behavior problem for her mother, father, and stepmother. Though her father repeatedly invited her to join him and his wife on many of the trips they shared together, the girl was always sullen and negative. Finally, her father took her on a short trip without his wife. "That little girl came back a new person," reported the psychologist. "She needed to know that she still had a direct line to her father."

A stepmother should not begrudge an emotionally needy child extra parental time and attention, as long as the needs are real. (The trouble comes with a child who demands that his father and stepmother sublimate their own interests to accommodate him.) However, a vacation is probably not the best setting for the extra attention that a deeply troubled stepchild needs. For everyone's sake, a vacation should not be confused with a therapy session.

Often private time for father and child that reaffirms their relationship is as essential as private time for a couple. It, too, should be part of any family vacation. In family vacations, loaded with so many considerations, parents may have more of an agenda than they would like, but that's the nature of the remarried life—and another argument for taking at least part of your vacations without children.

14

Holidays

olidays are the biggest reminder that a woman shares her husband with a family. Because a father and his children have a history of holiday traditions, the stepmother may end up feeling left out. For example, if he and his kids like oyster dressing at Thanksgiving but she prefers sage, she'll be outvoted. She'd better put both on the menu. This sounds petty—obviously, no sane person's holiday is made or ruined by the dressing—but superficialities take on symbolic meanings at holidays. Solutions that can please both sides are a good bet.

The same features that complicate and constrict family vacations often surround holidays. Both are short, finite periods of time to which people bring high expectations and emotions. However, holidays contain sentimental reminders of life before the divorce that tend to make them especially hard on stepfamilies, especially children. "They are reminders that the family is broken," note psychologists June and William Noble in their book *How to Live with Other People's Children*. Stepchildren can still remember the way holidays used to be. A stepmother who is doing her best to cope and to please everybody is still likely to get the impression that her best isn't in a class with the good old days. She shouldn't expect too much from herself or her stepchildren.

Women who are determined to re-create a happy home are doomed to disappointment because nothing can live up to a child's memories of a former unified, happy home. Even if it wasn't so happy, a child may recall it that way, and a stepmother simply cannot revise sentimental history. A holiday in your home might exceed the past in elegance, fun, comfort, sharing, or festivity, but it cannot put Mom and Dad back together again or create the atmosphere of the home that is broken, which is what all children want.

Stepmothers shouldn't knock themselves out trying. The best you can do is share your holiday spirit and welcome your stepchildren into it. Both you and your stepchildren suffer if your expectations are too high. Noncustodial stepchildren often have festivities at home on the actual holiday, so making too much of a fuss for them at your house can seem to pressure them to perform for your sake or to accentuate how much times have changed. Each family has its own traditions about tree decorating, gift exchanges, candle lighting, meals, etc., and most of us are reluctant to change them. While you're entitled to establish some traditions of your own, it's wise to ask stepchildren to contribute some of their own to your festivities.

Be specific. If you're set on colored tree lights but they used only white ones in your husband's former family, don't assign tree decorating to them. But if your stepchildren are spending Christmas with you this year, you might let them choose the dinner they'd like or contribute a favorite family dessert. There is always room for one more symbol or gesture at holidays. As is true of stepmothering in general, there is a gentle art to eliciting your stepchild's participation in areas where she feels comfortable and that you also welcome and enjoy.

GIFTS

Holiday gifts often pose problems for stepmothers. First, there is the opening of presents. You and your husband might prefer a stepchild to open a gift with you, but the child would prefer to save it for festivities at home. Sometimes it happens the other way around. You may want a present to go home, to be part of the child's "real" Christmas or gift exchange, but a child may feel awkward about opening a gift from you at home. The latter sounds like a father and stepmother's plea for legitimacy, to be symbolically present at occasions that exclude them. That's understandable, but the motive isn't worthy, and you are well advised to oblige the wishes of your stepchild. If opening your gift at home on Christmas morning creates tensions with the child's mother or is awkward for any other reason, forget it. The last thing a stepmother wants is to have her gestures tainted with unpleasantness. Ask stepchildren what they prefer regarding gift exchanges and don't let your happiness depend on their answer.

EXCESS

Holidays disturb stepmothers for more personal reasons as well. Because they glamorize family life, a stepmother commonly feels guilty. She blames herself and her marriage for obstructing the "big happy family." To compensate, she often feels obliged to put on a holiday presentation for her husband and his children. Uncertain about what she should do for stepchildren over the holidays, she plans festivities to the hilt—the way she thinks ideal mothers do. The responsibility is a bit overwhelming. She's more than an instant mother; she's an instant matriarch.

Jamie and her husband had been settled in their new apartment for only three days when her college-age stepdaughter, Amy, arrived for Christmas. Jamie said, "I'd kind of thought we'd have a quiet time together, but suddenly my mission was to make Christmas a big celebration. The low-key approach no longer seemed appropriate for my stepdaughter's homecoming." Jamie had been planning to be part of a festive twosome, but she found herself performing as a mother, responsible for every detail. "I felt that Amy and my husband were the real family, that I was just the director of events. I didn't feel as if it was really my place. My husband sort of left me in the lurch, but I don't think he knew what I had to do. He'd never been in charge of a holiday; he just expected it to materialize. A mother's place needed to be filled, and I was the best candidate."

Tensions overtook the threesome when Amy monopolized her father while Jamie worked away on a turkey dinner in the kitchen. When Jamie emerged to join the conversation, Amy said, half in jest, "Oh, just go back and make your turkey." Said Jamie, "I fumed. The martyred-mother's part didn't suit me. I saw Amy as the reason my holiday was a wreck, and I resented her."

It's easy to see why stepchildren and stepmothers are in opposition over holidays—they want different things. A stepchild wants a home-styled Christmas with an attentive father. A stepmother wants a private, special occasion with her husband. Both must compromise—but not sacrifice.

With precise planning, one couple mastered a method for heading off holiday tensions. "My husband's kids either come the week before Christmas, for Christmas, or for New Year's, but not for all three. They can choose when it will be, whatever works with their plans. During their stay we plan a lot of festivities, a celebratory dinner, shopping, a night out, a lot of fun things. We bake, we decorate, we do the whole thing. It doesn't matter whether it is actually Christmas Day or not. And I know that when it's over, some holiday time is still reserved for us. I enjoy having them so long as I know some occasion without them is protected," said the stepmother.

When stepchildren travel from afar to spend the holidays with you, it's less practical to reserve a piece of a holiday occasion for a couple, but plans for a private weekend getaway or winter vacation to look forward to can help a couple feel that there's something separate ahead for them. It can also do wonders for a stepmother's flagging morale. Swaps, trade-offs, compromise, and preplanning are the name of the game when mixing family togetherness with marital tranquillity is the objective.

PLANNING

Such careful orchestration and planning, though essential to successful stepfamily holidays and vacations, unquestionably sacrifice some spontaneity and ease. Well, you can't have it all. Stepfamilies without tensions and with low expectations may be able to manage their affairs without programming, but the evidence suggests that poor planning and lack of control are the greatest threats to holiday harmony.

"When my stepson phones and says he wants to come and bring a friend for Thanksgiving, I always hesitate. I wish that I didn't, but I do. I struggle with two reactions. I want to say, 'Sure, come. The door is always open,' but at the same time I feel myself become defensive. Wait, I think. Is this what we want for this holiday? Am I up to the preparation, the imposition? So I always sound wishy-washy about plans. I don't want to get locked in until we confer. I always say I'll get back to him. The process makes me feel guilty. I wish I could be more straightforward," a stepmother said.

Yet when she and her husband do extend themselves to her stepson, she feels happy about the gesture, not as though she's been stampeded into it. That's an important difference for everybody. "Spontaneity may be difficult since issues of time, money, and commitments are always shared elsewhere in remarried families," notes Clifford Sager, in encouraging stepmothers to accept this feature of stepfamilies. Furthermore, he and his coauthors of *Treating the Remarried Family* also remind remarrieds to be wary of the toll that stepfamily management can take: "Attempts at masterminding schedules, personal priorities, and family events drain energy and lead to frustration." These are hard realities. So stepmothers should not feel flawed by their mixed and sometimes negative reactions to holidays.

Stepmothers often get miffed when their stepchildren forget to remember Father's Day or their husband's birthday. They somehow feel that they are their husband's protector. Usually, these remembrances have more significance to you than to your husband. "I was so furious that I cried when my stepson forgot my husband's birthday. But my husband couldn't understand what the fuss was about. He said his son always forgot—he expected it. A month later, he received a card and laughed about it. I just didn't know what the pattern was, and I wanted everything to be perfect for my husband. It was important to me that he get his due as a father. I didn't want to feel he was missing anything because of our life," a stepmother said.

GETTING TOGETHER

Getting the gang together for birthdays or other celebrations always seems to make a stepmother feel good about herself and her part in the family. But failure to bring off these get-togethers as planned, such as a child's refusal to put in an appearance or to cooperate when he is there, can be extremely frustrating. Before you try to orchestrate a family gathering, ask yourself if the occasion is a realistic reflection of your family relationships. Don't use it to force a stepchild into a conciliatory or affectionate position that he or she doesn't feel comfortable with.

If you and your stepchildren are barely on speaking terms at the moment, planning a party together can exacerbate friction and make you both feel worse. When existing relationships aren't easy or flexible, it's unwise to be too ambitious. You can successfully celebrate a birthday or special occasion without having a whole family in attendance. Take the honored family member out to dinner or have a fancy lunch in the neighborhood where you or your husband work. Opt for an air of cozy festivity instead of grand scale to preserve a sense of occasion. If you're uncertain about what a child's response would be to a cooperative effort or get-together, plan something small, such as a dinner, that can be canceled or rescheduled without a lot of disappointment or trouble.

The other extreme, denying stepchildren any part of your holiday plans, is equally wrong. The stepmother who makes holiday plans without taking her stepchildren into consideration, pretending that she and her husband are as footloose as a childless couple, is just as bad. Either attitude will transform a holiday into a hardship.

NOT GETTING TOGETHER

In some families, the strains and sadness that accompany holidays are so severe that a radical departure from old habits is recommended. Clifford Sager explains that "family milestones (holidays, birthdays, and such), rather than being experienced as occasions where bonding is enhanced, may instead heighten feelings of loss, sorrow, and divided loyalty." For everyone's sake, remarried couples shouldn't get locked in to old patterns that don't suit their situation. Spending time in neutral territory, a country inn, or some other vacation spot, can provide a needed change of scenery for everyone.

When a child's distress at traveling between two households is evident, then it's time to consider spending a holiday season apart. But such a solution frequently casts a pall on a father's spirits. To help, a stepmother may need to create a distinctive holiday pattern for herself and her husband. She should initiate new traditions and wholeheartedly help to recover lost time with the child on another occasion. A weekend after the holidays could be a better, less emotionally loaded time for everyone.

"During these emotionally laden times there's no sense inviting your stepchildren if it's going to be miserable for them or for you. Why celebrate if it causes more conflict?" maintains Thomas Seibt. He recommends that stepfamilies "get rid of the 'shoulds.' I try to give people a lot of permission to do what works best for them, not what society tells them (often wrongly) works best for a different kind of family."

15

Money

"If I could just keep my husband from opening his checkbook, I think everything would be okay," said Abby, a stepmother whose financial story is the worst that I have heard. It deserves telling because it is the nightmare most of us dread.

Abby's husband, a lawyer, wrote his own divorce agreement ten years ago. He committed himself to generous child support, the full cost of prep schools and college educations, even the finest sporting equipment for all of his children's sports. (They bought everything from hockey sticks to polo ponies before his obligation was met.) Shortly after their marriage,

Abby and her husband moved to a less expensive neighborhood, sold their boats, and gave up boating, their favorite recreation, in order to meet his financial responsibilities to his children. "My husband would give them anything to purge his guilt for leaving them. I love him, but I would never put myself through this again," she stated. They postponed having a child of their own so that Abby could keep her job and contribute to the strained family budget. Though her husband's ex-wife married a millionaire, Abby and her husband kept making substantial personal sacrifices in order to meet the expenses of the children. "Because their mother lived in such luxury, nothing their father did ever seemed good enough," Abby continued.

Even fathers who practice law probably shouldn't draw up their own child-support agreements, since emotion (guilt) is likely to outweigh legal objectivity. Another lawyer would probably have protected his client's interests better.

Too much generosity is often as bad as stinginess. The more remarried couples strain to give at their own expense, the more they're likely to expect in return, which is asking for trouble. A stepmother and father who expect to be paid back in affection or achievement in proportion to the money spent upon stepchildren are asking for—and deserve—disappointment.

"I began with such commitment to them. We gave them birthday parties and presents from day one. I shopped for their clothes, put on holiday celebrations. I wanted to do it then, but now I resent that we have given up so much for them and they have turned out so poorly," stated Abby. Though her stepchildren are now young adults and mostly self-supporting, they continue to call collect and ask for handouts. Her resentment deepened when they overlooked her husband's fiftieth birthday this year. "Not one of them so much as sent him a card. I called each of them to remind them. I even offered to pay their plane fare to get them here, but the day passed without a word. That hurts the most. They take a man I respect and show him no respect at all."

Obviously, more than money is at the root of this stepfamily's difficulties. Unresolved guilt, misplaced priorities, and lack of discipline translate into financial troubles. When money is considered to be the solution to other problems, it's likely to *become* the problem. The behavior of Abby's stepchildren is a poor return on the financial investment she made, and their thanklessness adds insult to injury. Their stepmother is powerless to prevent the insult, but she could have minimized the injury. The realization that she and her husband shouldn't have given so much was a bitter pill to swallow.

Professionals preach over and over again that the standard of living, especially if a father provides support for all family members, will be lowered for everyone in remarried families. The ex-wife and children receive (notice that I do not say *have*, which is often a different story) less than before, a husband has less to keep, and his marriage has less money to operate with than it would if it were unfettered by stepchildren. Fathers stand a chance of easing the family financial strains if their earning power increases in the future, and a working stepmother can have a real impact on the finances of her household, but both households—not just the father's—should reflect the new financial reality.

Attempts to support the children beyond one's means are not realistic, and they may breed resentments and marital troubles like Abby's. A father's contribution should accurately reflect his financial situation. Even if his ex-wife becomes fabulously wealthy, money should not be permitted to become a competitive sign of his concern for his children. The temptation will always be there. Tensions over money will probably always be there. Money causes conflicts in all families and marriages. "In stepfamilies, however, money can take on many emotional overtones," state Emily and John Visher, who advise couples to separate their financial and emotional problems and address them individually.

Extreme cases may call for professional help to untangle the emotional problems from the financial and solve them separately. In less convoluted family money matters, the shared experiences and solutions of others—the kind of thing available in support groups—can be extremely useful.

Abby finally broke through some of the financial frustrations and barriers that she and her husband had created over the years when her youngest stepson came by last fall to tell his father that he planned to drop out of college. "My husband's heart was broken. He begged him to stay in school," Abby said. At the end of the evening she took a different approach. She took her stepson aside and laid the financial situation on the line. "I told the boy to remember that his father had heart trouble, and that if he died before the boy decided to return to college, as far as I was concerned, the boy's right to an education would be forfeited. I wouldn't pay for it." The next morning her stepson announced he was returning to school after all.

Abby's story is an extreme case, but money matters are a major issue for almost all stepmothers. For her part, a stepmother must reexamine her familiar old enemy: expectations. Chances are she didn't investigate her husband's financial commitments before she married him. Money is often considered too sensitive and unromantic a subject to discuss before marriage. Talking over what a man pays in child support and alimony seems an even more distasteful topic. A wife-to-be is more likely to know about her future husband's previous sex life. Yet sooner or later a second wife must understand his financial position so that her own expectations will reflect reality. Will her husband's ex-wife share the cost of her stepchildren's higher education? Does a husband plan for his children to attend private schools at his expense? These are just a couple of the questions that need to be answered.

For many men, their ability to provide is a test of their manliness. One stepmother was aghast when her husband arranged to take her through his ex-wife's fashionable home. He lived in a modest studio apartment at the time. "He wanted me to see what he was capable of providing, what his home had once been," she remarked. It was so important to him that she went, albeit reluctantly.

Avoiding financial questions and issues only causes distrust and insecurity between marriage partners. Prenuptial agreements may not be necessary or attractive for many couples, but even where they do exist, they don't replace open and honest financial discussions. Wise remarried couples also realize that wills, home titles, and life insurance are often not clear-cut and neatly protected in remarriages. Both partners should make an extra effort to ensure that their interests—and the interests of their children—are legally protected against tangled claims.

Family law experts have also discovered that legal circumstances are more likely to change with time in stepfamilies. For example, a new stepmother and her husband may want to revise their wills after they have a child or after an ex-wife remarries. If finding appropriate legal advice is a problem, family law departments in state law schools generally can refer you to the right place.

I can't say that I've liked the financial obligations my husband has had to his children and ex-wife; I'm sure we could have found ways to put that money to work for us. Yet I accepted them with relative ease (though not with total equanimity) because I knew from the beginning what the cost of his former family was going to be to him. It fitted in to my projection of our future. People often ask me if these financial obligations trouble me. It's something that people are curious about, that they think about when they see a stepfamily. During a tight spot, when my husband and I were paying for two college educations, I must admit I complained a bit, but I had no right to do so because I had been forewarned. Rather than being at odds with him, I felt like his earning partner, and a contributor to my stepchildren, and I took some satisfaction in that. That may be egocentric, but it's better than feeling like a victim.

The irony of stepfamily finances is that stepchildren often earn less of their own way than do children in nuclear homes. If money is a battleground between ex-spouses, as it often is, mothers may teach their children that they are entitled to financial advantages and need not earn them. Most stepmothers would argue that a child's character is sacrificed in order to get a few extra dollars from his father.

A stepmother can help her family by keeping financial matters in perspective and calming down other family members who may become dominated by emotion. Money is bad business if it's used as a weapon to spite an ex-wife or a new wife. Don't compete with an ex-wife by trying to outdo what she spends on the children. Work to increase and protect your own family accounts by earning or budgeting, but stay out of negotiations between your husband and his former family, except as his behind-the-scenes confidante. When a husband provides the sole or primary support for his children and ex-wife, be prepared for pettiness and hassles. There may be no money for train fares, shoes, whatever. People, and maybe ex-wives especially, become theatrical over money matters.

Stay clear of money squabbles with your stepchildren, too. You can be certain that they resent having their parents wage financial battles through them. The child who is made to ask when the child-support check is likely to arrive probably hates asking more than the father hates hearing it. It only makes matters worse if you ridicule her mother. If you're accused of buying $500 shoes while they're on food stamps, you can be forgiven for setting the record straight. Otherwise, stay clear of money battles. Most stepmothers see enough pettiness over money to make them want to renounce worldly goods entirely.

Sometimes in stepfamilies, generosity pays. " 'My husband's ex-wife was on us constantly about money," stated a stepmother who was resentful at how pinched she and her husband were while his ex-wife had more disposable income than they did. Then her stepson, who was in the sixth grade, ran away from home. "His mother called and said she didn't want him. I was so appalled that a mother would say such a thing that I told my husband we should do whatever we could to improve the situation. Some things are more important than money. We managed to put enough together to send him to boarding school, to try in every way to show that we cared about his welfare and that we hadn't abandoned his mother with her problems. We wanted it known that we cared and would offer emotional and financial support where we could. And you know what? She's splitting the school bills, and things are a lot better with her. Once she could see that we were behind her and concerned, things were okay."

As with the rest of stepmothering, there is a thin line between enough and too much. Even generosity can be taken too far.

Kids don't respect a brimming pocketbook any more than they
do those special gifts and dinners that they suspect are tendered
to manipulate them. If your budget permits, you may give a gift
or buy the skirt that you think any college freshman should
have, but remember: it's *your standard* that you are pleasing. If
your stepchild's personality is open to your influence, some of
your values may take hold, but don't strain your finances trying
to put your stamp on a stepchild's experience. The jacket you
scrimped to finance that always ends up on the floor obviously
meant more to you than to the child who received it. Ultimately,
it costs you even more in the way of aggravation. Don't go shopping for irritation.

Possibly the best contribution that a stepmother can make to
her stepchildren in money matters is her sense about money. A
stepmother's values are often different from their mother's. A
stepmother who believed her stepdaughter to be "extraordinarily spoiled" spent a good part of the drive to a family ski holiday convincing the girl to buy secondhand skates and to stretch
a cash gift by budgeting. The stepmother said, "She doesn't get it
from anywhere else. She told me that her mother has a hundred
pairs of shoes and models herself after Alexis Carrington on
Dynasty." The stepmother hopes her financial training will
soak in.

Ex-wives, because they have a legal hand in the till, figure
largely in the financial picture of a remarriage. Sometimes stepmothers wonder who are worse, ex-wives who have or those
who have not. While one stepmother and her husband struggled
to set up housekeeping in a small apartment and her husband
relocated in a new law practice, his ex-wife remarried and
moved to an affluent suburb, drove a Mercedes, spent weekends
on her new yacht, and put a pool in the backyard. And all the

details were recounted in full by the stepchildren. Still, their father was legally required to make child-support payments, which he and his wife took out a bank loan to cover. "I was strapped because of them, yet she lived in luxury," moaned the stepmother. Comparisons are even crueler and more unsettling for stepmothers with children of their own who must live with the leftovers after child-support and alimony payments. The world is full of people who have more than you, but when they're in the same family or when they get a chunk out of your budget, the contrasts are harder to take.

A stepmother is unlikely to have any control over how money is spent in her stepchildren's household—even if she helps to earn it. One stepmother I know says she used to "go crazy" when her stepchildren arrived in expensive shoes. Her own children wore moderately priced footwear, and she left her children at home with a baby-sitter while she worked to keep everyone financially afloat. Her husband's ex stayed home. It infuriated her, but there was nothing she could do about it.

Worse yet, some mothers don't always spend child-support money for a child's upkeep. Stories about the stepchild who doesn't receive the allowance or clothing that child support is ostensibly designed to provide for can be aggravating, even heartbreaking, when a child is obviously needy. A mother intent on putting the money elsewhere can usually claim that it went into home maintenance. Only the most extreme misuses, grounds for finding a mother unfit in court, would legally require an accounting. A stepmother and her husband raged when his ex-wife put her court settlement into a silicone breast implant rather than her home or children. They definitely have cause to be furious, but legally, it was the mother's own business.

A stepmother who lobbied to get her stepdaughter to buy a

moderately priced bicycle during her summer visitation period was undermined when the girl's mother instructed the girl over the telephone to buy "nothing but the best." The mother even said that she would pay the difference in price between "the best" and her stepmother's choice. Fair enough. The girl bought the bike, but the mother never offered to reimburse the stepmother for the difference, despite several gentle reminders. Finally, the father withheld the money owed from his monthly child-support payment. His ex-wife threatened to sue and had her lawyer phone him. "This woman does this just to harass him. She phones her lawyer every time she has a headache," the stepmother said.

There are some legal grounds—misconduct or changed financial circumstances, for instance—for modifying divorce agreements, but it is difficult to generalize about them. Laws and legal attitudes vary from state to state. The good news is that most courts and judicial attitudes are being updated. At one time a mother was always considered right—and needy. Now it is more often assumed that a divorced mother will contribute to her children's livelihood if circumstances permit. "There has been a complete revolution in family law," states Professor Homer H. Clark, Jr., of the University of Colorado Law School, author of the textbook *Domestic Relations in the United States*. "All the old notions of how families ought to work and how people ought to behave have completely broken down," asserts Clark, in explaining the trend toward custom-made divorce and child-support agreements. Almost half of all cases on civil court dockets are family law cases. Research findings indicate that people are more likely to go to court over post-divorce disputes today than they were in the past, and one study from the University of

Wisconsin Law School found that 60 percent of those with post-divorce problems went to court.

It's worth remembering, though, that going to court costs money, and the outcome is uncertain. Out-of-court agreements are invariably preferable to family law solutions, and less expensive, but courts definitely have a more flexible interpretation of family law than they once did. Dr. Doris Jonas Freed and Henry H. Foster wrote in the *American Bar Association Annual* last year: "In general, we are agreed that dead marriages should be buried, that family assets should be fairly divided, that the economic circumstances should govern alimony or maintenance, and that children, where possible, should know and associate with both parents."

Money matters have a more direct impact on stepmothers with children of their own. "I didn't care a lot until our baby was born. It was my husband's business what he owed them. Now I see it as money that could be put to use for our child," said a relatively new mother. Professionals warn stepmothers against thinking of finances this way. Start by thinking of your husband's earnings as what he has *after* he's paid alimony and child support. You don't have to like it, but you have to accept it.

If you're having a lean year, stepchildren may have to forfeit camp or a ski trip, extras that they'd forfeit in an unbroken home during a lean period, too. Your stepchildren's financial portion of the family budget should reflect the reality of your money situation. You or their father can discuss it with them. Occasionally, straight talk about money matters can lend reality to what one stepmother calls "the Depression-days blues" that her stepchildren hear from their mother at home. Let their father tell them what child support and alimony he pays to their mother if they are getting a different story at home. Money should not be treated as a secret or as an emotional issue with stepchildren. Talk about it as a commodity that is in greater supply some times than it is in others.

Even childless stepmothers slip into funks because they start to count what goes out to the stepchildren and to imagine what that money could mean to their lives. It may be unattractive, bourgeois, greedy, and selfish, but it's also human and most of us have done it. But doing it too often may be hazardous to step-family relationships—and your mental health.

Said a stepmother who has a flourishing career and is married to a man whose achievements and professional status equal her own, "My husband and I are as successful as any of our friends, but we don't own anything. We have a lot less. His old family has the house, the cars, the security. We have nothing." But nothing has changed since she married him. Clifford Sager, in *Treating the Remarried Family,* explains the monetary differences between nuclear and remarried families: "Comparing and contrasting nuclear and remarried families inevitably leads to exaggerations in which the nuclear family is idealized and the remarried family appears as a situation so trouble-filled that it is to be avoided. Neither polarized end is totally accurate."

Granted, it's easier to see your friends or neighbors surpass your standard of living than it is to watch your stepchildren and their mother live lavishly off income partly contributed by you, but a woman who takes a cold hard look at the joint financial picture from the start runs less risk of being disappointed later. Also, let's not forget that your stepchildren have genuine needs, and their father has a responsibility to care for them. They must be clothed and dressed. They must have a roof over their heads. What does it cost to run a household? And his ex-wife is probably entitled to something for their years together, even if you think it may be less than what she receives.

On the bright side of finances, stepchildren do grow out of the nest (and the budget), and they even graduate from college eventually. Ex-wives sometimes remarry. Time alleviates many stepfamily financial responsibilities, and time is on your side. Also, for the working woman, her contribution can have a considerable effect on her household's financial picture. Here's a place to bang the drum for the working woman, who can take genuine pride in her earning capabilities—a sense of worth that ex-wives who refuse to work often deny themselves.

A stepmother I know became so exasperated hearing from her stepchildren that they and their mother should receive more money because "Mom can't find work" that she marched out and found a job as a park employee in a nearby national forest. Her prospective employer agreed to let her take her nursing infant along on the job. "I did it purely to show those kids that when you are able-bodied and you want a job, you can get one. Their mother doesn't want one. She'd rather take more from us, and now her children know it," she said.

Some stepmothers follow the opposite course. In a stepfamily under financial stress, the stepmother told her husband, "I'll work when your ex-wife does." Meanwhile, they scrape along, though the stepmother has her principle. The ex-wife manipulates this case expertly. Every time her ex-husband tries to interfere in the discipline or upbringing of his children, she asks for more money, as if he must buy his parental involvement. It's ugly and small-minded. If money is perceived as power and the stepmother wishes to increase hers, she might bend her principle a little and make life easier by working.

"Money struggles often bring out the worst in everyone con-

cerned: husbands, wives, and attorneys. These battles are motivated by reality and emotional factors—fear, humiliation, anger,
revenge, avarice, territoriality, guilt, and chauvinism," states
Clifford Sager. He goes on to say that stepmothers should "deal
with money as a reality, not an emotional issue."

Money definitely helps ease stepfamily problems. Hired help,
camps, vacations, nursery school, therapy, baby-sitters, household
accommodations, and education choices, when affordable, can
greatly alleviate strains on a stepmother. Yet studies show lower-
income families have better stepfamily relations because they are
more accustomed to taking in extra family members.

If money were the heart of the matter, no woman would
marry a divorced man. However, most second marriages are
more likely to be affairs of the heart. Most people, romantics in
particular, believe that couples who have other (some might say
higher) values than money can overcome financial obstacles.

Money matters shouldn't dominate the mood of remarriage
and stepfamily life. In short, don't let them discourage you.
Though some money worries and hassles are probably unavoid-
able, many can be overcome or minimized so that they don't
overshadow positive things. Clifford Sager concludes, "The
goodness in these relationships usually makes the difficulties
worthwhile."

16

Family Gatherings

Family affairs—those sometimes warm, often stressful times when the whole clan is expected to be together—cause special complications for stepfamilies. Any occasion that mixes you and your husband's ex-wife and at the same time puts all your family relationships on display is sure to cause uncertainty and discomfort. It can certainly get your adrenaline pumping.

Everyone must recognize and learn their roles in the new family hierarchy, and they are definitely not like *The Waltons'*. (*Dynasty* might be more like it.) The relationship between you and your husband's ex-wife determines the ease or anxiety that characterizes most family affairs.

Some former wives and stepmothers show a surprising ability to work together for a relaxed atmosphere, but they are not yet the norm.

"My husband's ex-wife came down and stayed overnight with us during my stepson's graduation weekend. Our friends thought it was pretty weird, but it wasn't, really. She and I get along decently, and my husband is married to me, not her, so why should I let her bother me?" asks a stepmother whose relationship with her husband's ex is unusual. Most of us are a long way from having such an ideal arrangement, easy and uncomplicated for both sides and congenial for the kids. Either we are unwilling to work together this closely or the former wives are. Often our husbands are excruciatingly uncomfortable, and our stepchildren all but break out in hives.

Family psychologists all seem to raise an eyebrow when the subject of relationships between stepmothers and ex-wives is broached. They look to these relationships for a future breakthrough in stepfamily relationships. In recent years they have observed a slight shift toward cordial and cooperative relations that used to be rare. As a professional pointed out, it was once an unheard-of practice for divorced partners to act civilly toward each other. Now they frequently do. Being in each other's company is a concession more and more women make for the good of their families and children.

Being seated on the same blanket at a fireworks display is about as close as most ex-wife-and-stepmother relations are expected to be. If those occasions seem strained, just imagine the sweaty palms that all partners, present and ex, develop over funerals, weddings, graduations, grandparents' anniversaries, and all manner of large family gatherings.

While some of the strains and lack of ease are mostly matters of pride and uncertain protocol, other frictions surrounding family affairs are more serious and disquieting. Funerals pose genuinely threatening dilemmas for a stepmother at a time when she is poorly equipped to deal with strain or dissension.

Thoughts about a husband's funeral often enter and disturb a stepmother's thinking. We hope that we will be accepted and have an unchallenged and irrevocable position in our stepfamilies by that time. Nevertheless, fears and fantasies about the final family and public recognition of our status do cross our minds.

"If anything happened to my husband, I couldn't go to the funeral," said a stepmother who feels in the minority within a family dominated by her husband's children and his former wife. "I'd be alone because they'd be a majority. He's mine now, but when he's dead, he'll seem like theirs." Again, maybe this is a valid emotional reaction, but it is not rational.

One stepmother who lived through such an ordeal told a surprising story. When her husband, twenty-seven years her senior, died, he was survived by his wife, Dee, twenty-five, and his six children, eighteen to thirty-two. Despite the narrow age differences, Dee felt, "I couldn't break down. I had to be the adult, the leader." And so she was. She made the funeral arrangements and orchestrated the wake with her husband's relatives. Her husband's ex-wife was invited, but according to Dee, "It was such a joke. She acted the part of the bereaved widow." When the ex cornered Dee at the wake and began to shower her with abuse, Dee's stepchildren intervened and hustled their mother home. One of her stepdaughters even made apologies for her mother's behavior.

Proper status at family affairs can take on symbolic significance for stepmothers. Social occasions less somber than funerals often pose similarly sticky moments and problems. Though it might be nice if proper etiquette for stepfamilies were engraved in stone somewhere and handed out in divorce court, I'm sure everyone would squabble over its interpretation anyway. The personalities involved must always be taken into account, and that's exactly the problem.

Judith Martin, in *Miss Manners' Guide to Excruciatingly Correct Behavior,* offers the best and most realistic advice. First she wisely pokes a little fun at these complications. Responding to queries about who can be seated next to whom at wedding-rehearsal dinners and in church pews, she admonishes: "Such silliness has got to stop." A wedding, she maintains, is not a set piece with rigidly prescribed roles. She advises brides to "rewrite the script to fit the company." I particularly enjoyed her suggestion that each member of a family should hire an agent so that questions of billing and roles could be worked out before a wedding.

However, her serious advice is that the bride choose one parental couple (currently married or otherwise paired) to send announcements and invitations and that natural parents, seated as they wish, do the formal honors during the ceremonies. She suggests that all parents and stepparents be on hand to receive guests. I would amend that a little. If I were the bride, I'd prefer having my own parents' names on the announcements. Mr. and Mrs. So-and-so is obviously not correct for a divorced couple, but Jane So-and-so and John So-and-so, even if the surname is still the same, lets both parents into the act and still states the difference if anyone is looking for it. It probably makes the bride feel better, and that should be a stepmother's objective.

I came hazardously close to getting snared in this mess of delicate sentiments as a bride, and I remember how tormented I was when my father suggested bringing the woman he was dating at the time. I didn't want her at my wedding as a host figure.

She wasn't my mother (who was dead). Now that the tables are turned, I can see that I was being foolish and somewhat small-minded, but it was my wedding and it mattered to me.

I also recall the wedding of a good friend of mine. She was the traditional sort, and her wedding was an exercise in classic elegance. When her stepmother arrived in a red velvet pants suit wearing a hat with a veil, gasps were clearly audible in the church. I still don't know what motivated that woman. It would have been funny in a Woody Allen movie, but in real life it was not. I would recommend that a stepmother go a long way toward accommodating her stepchildren in these situations. A little understanding will probably pay off later.

I don't suggest you bow out entirely. A stepchild can't expect you to be left with good feelings if you're excluded. Your husband, especially if he's footing the bill, would not like it either, but it's tough enough for children to wrangle with their natural parents over these events, let alone deal with a bickering committee of natural parents and stepparents. Don't be a martyr. Speak up if you think some plan is unrealistic or offensive; if you want some sort of recognition, seating arrangement, place in a receiving line, whatever, say so. Nobody else is likely to know any more about what's proper in these situations than you do. Beyond that, my advice is to take a backseat and enjoy your freedom from responsibility. Let the kids and their folks sweat it.

If you and your husband are paying for a social function, that, too, is a factor. When it comes to weddings and other high moments for stepchildren, an indulgent approach regarding the child's preference for arrangements is best, but if you're helping to pay for the party and you want to be there, go.

Reunions, weddings, and graduations—family events that mix members and also attach some kind of status to seating arrangements or functions of the host—cause stepfamilies the most anxiety. A few tips for stepmothers:

(1)   Assume that everyone is as uncertain and uncomfortable about these arrangements as you are. They would probably welcome hearing your preferences and ideas. One stepmother said: "My stepson's mother went to his graduation and my husband went, too, but I couldn't go because there were a limited number of seats available for family members. I missed being there, but I made up for it and felt like part of things by giving a little party for him afterward. We invited his mother. She didn't want to come, but I felt that I had done my duty by sincerely suggesting it to her, and my stepson seemed to think the arrangement was fair and realistic. We talked about it beforehand."

Stepmothers often mention being excluded from family gatherings because other family members feel awkward mixing ex and current wives. "When my husband's nephew was married, we weren't invited. But Delia, his ex-wife, was. She has custody of my stepchildren, and my husband's brother (the groom's father) wanted to be sure they would be there. I wanted our kids to be with the cousins, too. I was very hurt. My husband just shrugged it off, but later his brother apologized and said he hadn't known how to handle the situation. If we had spoken up and said we didn't mind attending with Delia, it might have been different," said one woman.

(2)   You can put people at ease and help guide them through awkward positions if you get a jump on the situation. Let them know if you don't mind mixing with your husband's

ex. If you feel uncomfortable about being there, say that you'd like your children to attend anyhow. Sometimes you can call an ex-wife yourself and test her opinion. If you both agree that you'd like to attend a certain affair, find a way to tell the host or hostess, who will undoubtedly be relieved to learn that you've worked things out yourselves. Act like a family member and don't anticipate being hurt by an oversight or misjudgment on the part of others. When you seem comfortable and assured, fellow family members are likely to take their cues from you.

"I told my mother-in-law that I expected she would stay in touch with my husband's ex-wife. They'd known each other ten years. Their relationship was nice for the kids, and it didn't bother me. She thanked me profusely for bringing up the subject because she said she'd felt strange about the new relationships. I also think she thought well of me for mentioning it. I didn't look small or petty," one stepmother reported.

(3) Keep in mind that some people—ex-wives, in-laws, and other family members—may not be ready for gracious relationships. Don't take their reticence personally or be insulted if everyone doesn't rise to the occasion you have in mind. If your suggestions are rebuffed or met with indignation, don't be angry or vindictive. You may consider them foolish, but it's best to ignore bad behavior and stay above one-upmanship.

(4) Don't ever make family affairs a place for competing or scoring points. It may not always be easy, but in the end you'll feel good about yourself and undoubtedly you'll be better regarded.

"Your emotional ties and the civility or lack of it among these people are legitimate considerations when you make your choices," says Miss Manners. I agree. But interpretation of civility is also suspect. One stepmother I interviewed said yes, her husband and his ex have a civilized relationship: "They don't use Colt .45s on one another. She can call him sometimes, and he's nice. They scream and yell. He hates her guts. I guess you could call it civilized."

Sometimes potentially awkward situations have a way of resolving themselves, and children often play a part. A stepmother who found herself seated in the back row during her stepson's Bar Mitzvah was dumbfounded when her stepdaughter came back and invited her to come sit up front with the family, in this case the girl's maternal grandparents and her mother.

In another case, a stepmother, her husband, and her stepdaughter's maternal grandparents and the child's mother all stayed in the same hotel in order to attend her stepson's graduation ceremony. "I asked my husband to arrange it so that our room was not next to his ex-wife's and that he and I would drive down to the university alone. Beyond that, I didn't care," the stepmother said. At first, relations were a little stiff among all family members, but then, to the stepmother's surprise, her stepdaughter's grandmother took the initiative to talk with her and to break the ice. The grandmother even invited her and her stepdaughter to go for ice-cream cones. "It was really very nice of that woman, and from then on it just seemed natural to be cordial to everyone. By dinnertime the tension was gone. We all sat at one table. I helped my stepdaughter order from the menu. She was sitting closer to me, and her mother was busy talking to her son. Under the circumstances it was pretty relaxed."

One way to ensure that these unusual occasions stay pleasant is to avoid using them to hash over differences or problems with your husband's ex-wife. This is not the time to get into issues of visitation schedules or anything else that you disagree about. Take up those topics at another time. Keep the conversation light and don't be thin-skinned. If you think some gesture or remark was intended to get your goat, ignore it.

Also, never challenge a mother's authority to discipline or correct her own child. She's the boss. You may have the final say about table manners at your house, but let them go at a family gathering. A mother is bound to take your criticism of her child personally, so defer to her whenever necessary.

Family affairs are meant to be pleasant, happy occasions. Your composure and your approach to them are crucial to ensuring that they will be—and to putting others at ease. Remember that almost all the uneasiness other family members feel about these affairs is focused on you and your husband's ex-wife. There is a certain irony in finding yourself at the center of these affairs, but it's understandable. You and the way that others respond to you are the most significant variables in a host of familiar, mostly long-term relationships. You'll get the most credit, and everyone will have a better time, if you help to put others at ease and work for the success of these occasions.

17
The New Family

To have a child or not to have a child—that is the question. And the answer can be more divisive than any other issue facing stepmothers and their mates.

There is a pattern. When they talk of their expectations and dreams, people who are about to be married are not always honest with each other. Or they simply change their minds, which is human, too. Early in a relationship stepmothers, especially childless ones, may mistakenly think that stepchildren will substitute for their own. Though they *said* they weren't hoping to have a baby later, once they learn that stepmothering is not like real mothering, and they are surrounded by peers who are having babies, their ideas change.

Husbands who once agreed to have a baby, "if you really want one," sometimes reconsider when they are faced with adding to their responsibilities. It may have been more a romantic statement of love than a heartfelt desire to begin another family.

Stepmothers who in their hearts secretly hoped to have a child but fudged the issue because their husband-to-be seemed overwhelmed with the responsibilities of children from his first marriage are guilty of the same brand of deception. They assumed their mate would change his mind or come around to their way of thinking. Other stepmothers, who originally felt neutral about having children, found that once they had tailored their lives to accommodate stepchildren, they might as well have one of their own to look after.

Remarriages frequently undergo one or more of these situations. "Men want marriage, so they bargain by saying, 'I'll give you a child,'" says Lillian Messinger. She warns couples that deciding to have a child in a second marriage when children are already present is "more complicated than deciding it in the first marriage. You both have to become closely involved in understanding what each other's hopes and needs are."

There's a larger chance here for mixed signals and conflicting emotions. The topic of having a child can greatly aggravate stepmothers, who may still feel vulnerable about being a "second" wife. Even those who decide to have a baby often harbor insecurities about whether their child will be as special or meaningful to their husband as earlier children. But they ought not to worry. Men who choose to have a second family cherish the second chance to treasure a baby and often to be more directly involved with nurturing than they were when their "first" chil-

dren were infants. The second time around a baby often reawak-
ens the whole joy of fathering in a man. Furthermore, many
babies of first marriages "just happened." Children of second
marriages are more likely to be the result of mature partnerships
and choice.

There is much to recommend bringing up a baby in a stepfamily, but only if you and your husband want it. Obviously, even
if a baby has a positive effect on the stepfamily as a whole, it's
not good for a stepmother or her marriage if it isn't genuinely
longed for. Otherwise the responsibilities and duties of motherhood would undoubtedly outweigh whatever positive effects a
baby might have on a stepfamily.

Sometimes, however, the complexities of stepmothering obscure or distort a woman's notions about parenting. It can be difficult for her to know her own mind and to make decisions
about becoming a mother in an atmosphere dominated by tensions or trouble. Stepparenting is not like parenting, and as
women repeatedly discover for themselves, it is not a substitute
for it either.

The issue of having a child taps many of the most primitive
desires and insecurities in any marriage. For the stepmother, it
invites comparison to the first marriage, and it can call into
question her husband's love of her and commitment to their life.
No matter how the question is ultimately answered, the process
of deciding will expose many truths about the partners and their
marriage.

"When I met my husband, he said that he'd be happy not to
have any more children, but if it would make me happy, he'd
have one more. I said I didn't know if I wanted children or not,"
remarked Marybeth. Two years into her marriage as the noncustodial stepmother of two adolescent boys, Marybeth, thirty-four

years old and feeling her childbearing years coming to an end, decided that yes, she wanted to have a baby. In the meantime, her husband had a change of heart: he said he really didn't want the responsibility of more children. Life in this household quickly went to hell. "For two years I have bent over backward for the children you've already had, and now you're going back on your word," Marybeth said to him. She recalled, "You could say I had a personality change. I absolutely hated him and his boys. I said, 'Don't tell me you love your sons. They are obviously more of a burden than a pleasure to you if you can't imagine having another.'" She, who once considered herself a model step-mother, announced: "Don't expect me to cook for them or make their beds or take them anywhere. They're your kids. You take care of them. I'm finished." Marybeth even told her parents, who regarded her stepsons as their own grandchildren, not to send them Christmas presents. "'The boys don't need a thing this year,' I told them. My heart just froze."

Then she played her last card. "I was intentionally casual about using my diaphragm, and I got pregnant," she said. When she told her husband, he responded positively at first. "It will work out. We'll love this child," he assured her. "Then," Marybeth said, "Grant became a basket case before my eyes. He never slept. He got up at 4:30 A.M. and went to work. Finally, he told me he couldn't go through with it, to get myself a lawyer and file for divorce. He said he hoped I would meet another, better man and try a new life. His parting advice was that I should have an abortion."

For the first time Marybeth understood how heavy a burden Grant's sons had been to him during his divorce and their remarriage. "There was fear written all over his face," she stated. As she awaited a scheduled abortion and contemplated a divorce from

Grant, their relationship became increasingly difficult. At his family reunion, which they dutifully attended together, she sat stonily and listened to Grant's toasts to his father, family, and fatherhood. "I just hissed 'hypocrite' at him in the car on our way home," she said.

Amazingly enough, Grant and Marybeth eventually patched up their relationship. Each of them became so afraid of losing the other when divorce actually became a subject between them that they decided to cancel the abortion and have their baby. Their story has a happy ending, but it took time. The same uncertainties and feelings that caused their discord over having a child characterized their new family relations. They had to work hard at resolving the underlying issues: his fear and lack of commitment to their baby as a consequence of his guilt, his unresolved feelings about his own sons, and her pain over his going back on his word.

As for stepmothering, having a child of her own renewed Marybeth's vigor for the challenge of caring for her husband's sons. As children frequently do, the boys rallied around the new baby. "It was heartwarming," she reported. One boy, who was handy at woodworking, made toys and nursery furniture in his shop class at school. Both brothers seemed genuinely involved and excited.

THE "OLD" FAMILY

A husband's reaction to his first children usually changes when a new child is born. A new baby can have a surprising effect. While you may turn all your maternal attention to this new child, freshly reexperiencing fatherhood often rekindles some men's commitment to and affection for their first children. They don't love the new baby any less, but the new joy reminds them of their early paternal responsibility and love.

Although this paternal reawakening is undoubtedly a genuinely loving and positive impulse, it can create problems in a stepfamily if it is mingled with guilt and uncertainty about existing father-child relations. It drives some fathers to extremes.

"My husband became Superdad," noted one stepmother. He flabbergasted her when he announced on Christmas Eve in the presence of his sons and her in-laws that the boys were leaving their mother to come live with him. The stepmother, five months pregnant, had not even been consulted. "I nearly fell over," she said. "I saw inviting the boys to live with us at that time as patently unfair, but he was fierce. He said that they were his boys, and he was going to keep loving them, and they were coming." Wrapped up in baby showers, Lamaze classes, and other aspects of pregnancy, she said she was "determined to be happy." She didn't want to argue, so she acquiesced.

When her stepsons moved in for the summer, her new son was two months old. Her husband was a doting new father, but this renewed role seemed mostly to remind him of what he'd missed with his older sons. "When he came home from work, I'd hear the car door slam and he'd be off with the boys to play tennis, baseball, or Frisbee," reported the mother, who was inside making dinner and nursing the baby. "I had a medley of emotions from joy to desperation." By summer's end she was in full-time therapy. At her request, her husband joined her.

"You won't believe me, but I think that today [two years later] he and I have one of the happiest marriages I know, but it took some work," she said. "My husband really had to uncover and examine a world of things about his feelings, guilts, and love for his sons before he was free to experience our child. I had to understand a lot and to accept a lot about what being a parent means to him and why he was so hesitant to begin again. I needed to be reassured that he loved me. We didn't talk nearly enough before we got married. We should have gotten help much earlier. He didn't know how traumatized he was about having more children. I never admitted to myself how much I wanted a baby."

MOTIVES

The previous story, a modern stepfamily romance, contains many elements that confront remarried partners who consider and decide to have a child. Though they may have had more than their share of complications, their opposing positions, reactions, and range of emotions are typical.

A stepmother married to a man with a vasectomy who said he would be happy to have it reversed if she ever wanted a baby resents how obtuse he becomes whenever she raises the subject. "I'm still unsure of what I want, but I've got to weigh the pros and cons in the full light of day and he just avoids it. He reasons that if the reversal is unsuccessful, I'll be disappointed. But I wonder what other course there is. We decide either to try or not to try. His reasoning is double-talk."

A frequent complaint from stepmothers is that husbands who obviously cherish their child or children nonetheless make the case that childbearing is "too burdensome, too much responsibility" to enter into all over again. "If having a child is so profound and wonderful, then why deny me that experience? It makes me feel as if he couldn't love our child as much," one woman said.

Comparisons and relative affection for a child are not really at

the heart of these arguments. Professionals report that unresolved guilt and fear of responsibility usually are. The feelings of
a husband who plainly and consistently says he doesn't want
more children should be taken seriously, but faulty and inconsis-
tent reasoning may warrant a closer and more earnest examina-
tion when the subject is such a serious issue. "My husband said
his daughter would be too threatened by a new baby unless she
came to live with us, too," one stepmother stated. Her therapist
helped her to understand her husband's "logic." "*He's* the one
who is worried over whether he could love them equally. He's
afraid of feeling more guilty toward his daughter."

If partners are at a stalemate over whether or not to have
a baby, a marriage counselor can provide invaluable help.
Sometimes just a dispassionate interchange with a disinterested
party can help. Because this issue carries far-reaching implica-
tions for a marriage, it's important that a couple reach a clear
decision based on true feelings and sensible reasoning. "It brings
so many thoughts to a conscious level," asserts Lillian Messinger.

Frequently the question requires that both husband and wife
take into account their separate life cycles to better understand
why each reacts as they do. A father of adolescent or adult children may feel that the parental stage of his life is drawing to a
close, while his wife, especially if she is younger, may be experiencing a newfound need to nurture. Both should examine and
discuss their feelings and hopes for their shared future. Neither
stage predetermines the outcome. An older father may feel more
financially secure and willing to have another baby in a happy
marriage. A young woman may be rooted in ambitions outside
the home, and she may not truly want children, despite the fact
that everyone she knows is having a baby. The point is that the
decision must be made in a frank and open atmosphere.

A stepmother with a successful career who was once determined not to have children said her resolve weakened temporarily because she felt jealous of her stepchildren. Now she has resumed her conviction, but she stated, "I'm glad I looked deeply enough into myself to see what was going on. I *really* don't want children. The turnaround came at a time in our marriage when I felt insecure. I wanted to feel more loved, and I thought a baby would help. I've learned other ways to find the love and affection I need."

STEPCHILDREN'S REACTIONS

When a baby does come into the stepfamily scene, it can affect stepchildren in many different ways. As in natural families, the arrival of a new baby can cause jealousy among older children. But a half sibling often has a positive rather than a negative effect on its siblings—and a stepfamily in general. The fact is, kids like a family; they like the security that adults provide and the hustle and bustle of other children. An only child, I remember the sense of well-being that used to come over me when I visited a friend who had five brothers and sisters. It was heavenly having so many things going on at once, not being the focus of attention. The same goes for stepchildren, who, despite natural varieties of sibling rivalry, are usually sucked into the family scene that a new baby creates. This family scene is often less threatening and more attractive to a child than straining to measure up socially in adult company with his father and new stepmother. It is plainly more fun. Ultimately, it is also liberating for a stepchild, because it takes the pressure off him.

It must be admitted that a new baby does pose threats to a stepchild—as does any other sibling. Those may be exaggerated in a stepfamily arrangement where a father and his child live apart, or where other insecurities affect the parent-child relationship. The personality and age of the stepchild are obviously crucial factors.

One woman told how differently her two stepdaughters reacted when her son was born. The younger, with whom she and her husband had developed a closer relationship over the years, really seemed to enjoy the baby. There was something special between them. The older, whose relationship with her father was less comfortable and resolved, was troubled. The baby was yet another factor to reckon with.

A psychiatrist whom the father consulted told him that his older daughter's reaction was wholly predictable: the oldest child is most likely to feel displaced—demoted—by the child of a second marriage. She is no longer unrivaled as the firstborn, an eminent position in families. Your new child, the fruit of a more current and vital partnership, challenges that supremacy. On the other hand, younger children are usually happy to be one more notch removed from being "the baby." I was repeatedly told of stepfamilies in which the youngest child of a first marriage drew close to the children of a second marriage. Even when the age differences were extreme, the new family provided a mechanism for straddling the gulf between two families. The impact of this realignment depends on the nature of the child, other disturbances in a household that may exist, and the parents' skill at anticipating and reckoning with them.

The older daughter confessed that watching her father play and love a new child hurt. She, like most stepchildren, needed assurance from him that their current relationship was secure, and that he was only giving the baby what he had once given to her—not withdrawing his love from her. Discussion seemed to do them both some good. Before they talked, she had felt tight and restrained toward him and the baby, and he could not help feeling self-conscious in her wounded and strained presence.

The biological link between these half siblings counts for something, too. Your children and your stepchildren have a blood relationship that circumvents even you. Sometimes it is uncanny. Stepmothers report that their own children, the new babies in these families, recognize and identify older half siblings as immediate family members even when they seldom see them. Without prompting from adults, they include them in their larger family picture and seldom seem confused as to who their siblings are.

Sociologist Lucille Duberman concludes in her study of remarried couples and their children, *The Reconstituted Family,* "The findings support the expectation that high family integration is likely to be found in those reconstituted families that contain a child from the new marriage." Obviously, having a baby is not recommended as a solution to stepmothering turmoil. The studies on which Duberman and others base their positive conclusions do not specify whether or not the "integration" that they speak of prompted the couple to add a new baby to the family, or whether the baby helped to create it. As Duberman notes, it is assumed that remarried couples are more cautious in general and probably felt good about their marriages and the chances for the continuing success of a larger family when they decided to have a baby. So babies are more often to be found in happier stepfamilies than in unhappy ones.

In families in which a stepmother also has children from a former marriage, a baby often unites both sets of older children by providing both sides with a common family member. Babies, creatures who appeal directly to all family members (even hard-to-please teens) and are innocent of the loyalty conflicts and guilts that adults and older children experience, sometimes help weld a stepfamily together. They also can lend a sense of stability and permanence to a couple, and that, too, draws stepchildren closer.

However, some stepchildren don't accept a new child unequivocally, and their attitude can polarize a stepfamily. When resentments prevail, a stepmother is sometimes tempted to see the family as teams: hers versus her husband and his. This is the wrong reaction. You and your husband have a child between you now, but he still has other children, and you and he must try together to help a child who is troubled by an additional family member to accept and cope with the reality.

Don't pressure a stepchild to love or dote on a new child. Settle for curiosity from him in the beginning and don't force the relationship between them. An older child (those adolescents again) may worry that he will have to babysit and that family life as he knows it will be ruined by the new baby. A friend of mine who was sixteen when her mother announced that she was having another baby remembers throwing herself on the couch and announcing that her life had been ruined. And that was in a nuclear family. So a stepmother shouldn't take it personally if her stepchild reacts negatively to the news of another child. Children are conservative by nature, and they often react defensively to any change in their lives.

There are many ways you can reassure your stepchild that a baby won't disrupt his or her world. Be certain he gets time alone with you and your husband without the baby's interruptions. Make an extra effort to set aside time for occasions that include him without the baby, such as a dinner out or a movie. You'll be busy, but don't start neglecting a stepchild because you have a baby. The extra effort to send cookies to camp or meet him at the bus terminal shows, in little ways, that you still care.

Also, babies and toddlers make their own appeals. Rather than trying to orchestrate a relationship under your direction, let the kids work it out on their own. A baby who makes eyes at its half sibling will get a more genuine reaction than any statement you can make. If the kids don't work it out on their own, don't despair. Lots of natural siblings don't either.

If your stepchild's reaction stays negative and hostile—more than just disinterested—get him some professional help. It's not wise to avoid the problem and hope that it will pass. A father needs to make the point that his concern is for his child and his good mental health—not over whether or not his child likes the new baby. As in most kinds of bad behavior, aggressive rejection of a half sibling is usually an appeal for attention. If a father can get to the bottom of his child's need, the reaction to the new baby will probably improve, too.

Mixing mothering and stepmothering does not get rave reviews from all quarters, though. "When my teenage stepson heard I was pregnant, he was horrible. He came over to tell me that abortions were available these days. I never forgave him," a stepmother said. "We waited a long time to have a baby, till my stepkids were well on their way in life. I'd done everything I knew to please them—birthday parties, family affairs, you name it. I can't tell you how it hurts to see them deny their half brother the affection that I showered on them." Her stepmother relations hit a new low when she found her four-year-old in tears because his half brothers and their cronies, all in their late teens, had mutilated his favorite doll. "I wanted to strangle them. For the first time I told them I'd had it with them and sent them home" she asserted. Her stepchildren's behavior problem is probably rooted in broader issues than the presence of a half sibling, but her anger is understandable when their malice is directed at her child.

YOU

One frustrated stepmother of two adolescents said, "I would have killed those boys a time or two except that they were so good to our daughter. They got up at night if they heard her crying. They loved to bring her toys and show her off. I forgave them all else and loved them for it."

Some stepmothers, those formerly without children, discover that their reaction to stepchildren who show affection to their children is more than simple gratefulness. They feel easier about stepmothering in general and less bewildered by parental duties. "If I was going to be caring for Jack's kids, hiring baby-sitters and carting them around on vacation—what I call 'kid life'—I figured I might as well have one of my own. With our baby I stopped resenting them," stated Ellen, who had a child two years after becoming custodial stepmother of a five-year-old. "When we had our child together, I felt I finally had what my husband had. I wasn't a fifth wheel anymore. Our time together was easier, more natural, no longer as though my stepdaughter was cramping my style." Custodial stepmothers such as Ellen experience the most direct change in their stepmothering relations when a new child enters the picture.

However, the bad news about mixing motherhood and stepmotherhood should be mentioned. Stepmothers-turned-mothers often feel that stepchildren encroach upon their time for mothering and the overall experience. Vulnerabilities over being a second wife and experiencing the romantic occasions of your life with his children on the scene can be troubling at such a tender time. Anxieties that your husband cannot experience the same joyful intensity of new parenting the second time around sometimes detract from your joyful anticipation. "My husband told Clare, my ten-year-old stepdaughter, that she could paint the secondhand crib that we bought for our baby. 'Make it your art project,' he instructed her. Well, I went berserk. This was *my* child, my first and probably my only baby. I wanted that nursery as pristine and perfect as could be. It *was not* going to be Clare's art project," a stepmother said. Her dictum about the crib won out, but she let things ride when Clare put their two cats in the baby's new buggy and strolled them through the neighborhood. "I didn't like it, but what could I do? If I forbade her everything, she'd be resentful of the baby, and I didn't want that. But I must confess that I catch myself wishing she weren't around, that I didn't have to contend with her at this period in my life."

Another custodial stepmother found, "Our baby is the glue to the whole picture. We all relate to Edward. I refer to him and my stepchildren as 'our children.' My husband has more confidence in my decisions regarding my stepdaughter now, and I don't feel as self-conscious disciplining her as I used to. I'm the mother here and that's it," observed this woman, who once had problems getting her husband to leave his daughter with a baby-sitter. Now she finds that he is less protective and trusts her judgment. "When we go out now, he and I are both leaving children we feel protective about. And we're leaving them together. It's much better." Many stepmothers also find disciplining stepchildren easier after they have a child of their own. "I never wanted to be the wicked witch before, but now I understand that setting rules

and enforcing them are just part of being a parent," said a stepmother of two and a mother of one.

A child of her own often works to raise a woman's consciousness about parenting and profoundly affects her response
to her husband's previous parenting. "I think the baby has sig-
nificantly affected the way I perceive my stepson. I'm more forgiving of him. Because I have a child I can better understand the
care and responsibility my husband shows him," a stepmother
reported. I agree. Once my husband and I had a child together,
I became more appreciative of his fathering and took pride in
things he did on his children's behalf, such as intervening during
an adolescent crisis or laying down the law about their grades at
school. Before, I had barely noticed. Suddenly, what kind of parent he'd been mattered a great deal to me. It was a model of how
he would be with our child. I also felt remorseful about times
when I'd been indifferent or difficult regarding his children. A
psychologist I saw during a troubled patch early in our marriage
had told me that despite my keen interest in legitimizing relations with my stepchildren, it was impossible for me to understand fully what he was feeling for his children. I didn't believe
her. Now I do. For me, the emotional complexities of parenting
changed from black and white to living color when I became a
parent, too.

Children and the reasons for having them are intimate and
emotional issues for any couple, but because a stepmother's husband by definition has fathered a child before, the subject can
become a cover-up for other frustrations, such as the inconven-
ience of stepchildren and those dreadful comparisons between
first and second marriages.

"Whether having a baby is a major conflict or not, discussion of it often becomes an occasion for acknowledging other resentments about stepchildren, money, what have you," cautions Thomas Seibt. "A woman who frequently feels that her husband is depriving her of a baby often feels bitter about other things that should be discussed, but the subject of having a baby becomes her focus." Because of this temptation to use a child— in fact or theory—as a weapon, stepmothers who feel emotionally troubled or volatile on the subject owe it to themselves (and any future child) to examine their motives thoroughly before they decide to begin a new family.

A child should be wanted for its own sake. It may have happy side effects for stepchildren and a stepfamily later. As many stepmothers know already, children who are born to score points in a marriage are likely to end up being stepchildren.

18

Custodial Stepmotherhood

Living with stepchildren is stepmothering in extremis. Noncustodial stepmothers, frazzled by the trickle of visiting stepchildren, often envy the constant authority of their custodial counterparts, but it's unlikely that the custodial arrangement is truly easier. Living with stepchildren can be less awkward than visitation, and the long-term relations that result may be closer and ultimately more rewarding; but the initial adjustment is undeniably more stressful.

Stepchildren's presence is a heavy and constant burden on a woman's marriage and daily routine. True, her stature in the family, as the woman in charge, is greater than when she is simply a weekend hostess. Still, the constant demands on a custodial stepmother are often overwhelming—like being swallowed *by,* rather than becoming part *of,* a family.

The circumstances under which a stepmother, her husband, and his children begin living together greatly affect the mood of the household that follows. A woman who was introduced to stepmothering when her husband took custody of his three young daughters away from his mentally infirm ex-wife had very special accommodations to make. "We all sat in a motel room. It was my job to comfort them, to give them confidence that everything would be okay. It was the most difficult task of my life," she said. Taking control in a crisis situation is certainly one of the most challenging ways to become a custodial stepmother.

This woman claims it's easier to begin living with stepchildren in chaos, when everyone is thrown together in the same rocking boat and must try to survive together. "The adjustment was hairy," she stated. "We had to begin life from scratch with many emotional problems and upsets, but we made it one step at a time." Obviously, much depends on individual circumstances. A stepmother isn't likely to have much choice about which situation she encounters. How she lives with her stepchildren will eventually matter much more than the manner in which they happen to end up under the same roof.

LATE ARRIVALS

A stepchild may come to live with the father some time after he and his wife have set up housekeeping as a couple. That adjustment can be greatly disruptive to a stepmother, but it may ultimately be to her advantage to have had some time alone with her husband and to be established as an operative head of their household before beginning full-time stepmothering.

If you never counted on living with your stepchildren, your biggest struggle may be to gracefully accept the turn of events that brings them to your doorstep. Children who are uprooted and moved about are invariably regarded with compassion and concern. The stepmother in these situations, too, deserves some sympathy. Despite her feeling for the children, her first reaction may be disappointment. And to complicate matters further, while she is adjusting to the new situation, she has to help her stepchild adjust to the new arrangement. One stepmother said, "My stepson didn't want to come here after his mother remarried. It was a pathetic situation. His mother didn't want him, and quite honestly I didn't want him to live with us. But he was coming and we were going to have to make it." Guilt and sorrow overcame her after she realized that her stepson had overheard her quarreling with her husband about him. "I had to set things straight, so I called him and my husband into the kitchen and told them that I was finding these adjustments very difficult and I was sure he was, too. The boy seemed to like my being straight with him. He agreed it was tough. We agreed to keep trying and to keep talking." Good often comes from sharing and discussing your mutual problems with a stepchild. According to the stepmother in this family, "When he and I did adjust and began to get along together, we shared a sense of accomplishment and success that was good for us."

HIS PLACE

Sue's teenage stepdaughters welcomed her with open arms when she married their father. They told her she was the best thing that had happened to him and that they were grateful to her. So as she prepared to move in to the house they shared with their father, she expected few problems. "We liked one another, and I assumed that I would take over as head of the house, that it would be my home, and that my presence would give every-one a boost," Sue said.

A month later, she had a different story to tell: "I felt like an outsider. Big and little things made it evident. The girls discussed upcoming weekend plans only with their father, as though I wasn't there or had nothing to say about them. They controlled who needed the car, whether friends were coming for drinks, whether we should eat on the porch, have Sunday brunch together, or sleep in. I just sat by and waited to see what was on the agenda." Eventually it was a little thing, an argument with one of her stepdaughters over what brand of toothpaste to buy, that made her feel panic and alarm. "It hit me when the eldest girl told me to buy Colgate toothpaste instead of Crest. She thought I should do things their way. For the first time I saw what I had gotten into. I had no authority. The girls were unyielding to all my suggestions, and I somehow felt like *their* child." Indeed, a major power struggle broke out when Sue tried to assert her authority.

The most difficult adjustment for a stepmother occurs when she moves in with a custodial father and his children. Invariably, even when her stepchildren like her, she is perceived as an intruder in *their* household. Children who live with bachelor fathers typically assume more adult responsibilities than those in traditional homes, and they are accustomed to having more say in the way things are done at home. A stepmother threatens that situation, and a child resents the change, even if he or she is, at heart, relieved to be freed of adult responsibility. A stepmother should expect some resentment, but she should not let it cause her to feel guilty or uncertain about her role in the family. It is right and proper that some power shift to her.

Don't overdo it or come on too strong at first, but state at the beginning that things are going to change in your stepchildren's house. You may decide to exert little control and make few changes until you've both adjusted to each other, but you need to announce that their lives will be changed by your presence, since they undoubtedly will, and saying so helps prepare children. When you do begin to take charge, it won't be such a shock. These small statements and symbols matter enormously in stepfamilies. A psychiatrist advised Sue to buy two kinds of toothpaste, her brand and theirs, to let her stepchildren see that she intended to do things her own way.

Your husband can be a big help in the beginning. A sensitive father can help reassure his children that his love and affection are constant despite the presence of a new authority figure. This is no time for a father to duck out and leave his new wife to manage on her own with his children. Loss of fatherly love is the primary fear of most children when a stepmother enters their household. Direction, patience, and sensitivity are essential on a father's part during this shuffling and realignment of household roles.

You can assuage other fears that your stepchildren may suffer. Tell them they'll be keeping their own rooms. Give them some indication of "what it will be like" living together. If you plan to have dinner alone with your husband several nights a week or to redo the dining room, prepare them for these changes in advance. If you and your husband have agreed to share setting rules and discipline, tell them. Take the surprise out of moving in together and don't assume that they understand anything unless you have spelled it out for them.

The relationships between stepmothers and stepchildren are neither automatic nor assigned. They must be achieved. A stepmother has to work at them. Those who passively wait for their stepchildren to address them with affection and concede them authority will have a long wait.

The combination of wanting to be linked *and* to be in charge trips up many women. It's comforting to know that even teachers, who confront this dilemma on a lesser scale in the classroom, are equally baffled by stepmothering. A woman with five stepchildren who is an educator and an assertiveness-workshop leader for her colleagues said she didn't know whether to laugh or cry when she confessed, " 'My biggest problem has been that the kids control the household. I do what they say. It has been so difficult for me to get in control. I want them to like me. They welcomed me warmly, but they resent me if I move a piece of furniture." In class, kids know that a teacher is the highest authority and will not hesitate to use her power. Stepchildren need to know that about their stepmothers, too.

Sometimes too much authority is as bad as too little. "It's as though my husband handed over his parenting to me. What a good deal I am for him," a stepmother said. A husband who is an active parent is a great asset to a stepmother, particularly a custodial one, whereas a husband who abdicates most of his parental duties with the advent of a stepmother needs to be reminded that his help is wanted—and urgently needed.

"My husband thought he was finally free to work late and take business trips after our marriage. 'Ah, at last the kids have a mother' was his reaction. So I had to level with him that I was beginning to hate six to eight every evening, when the kids were a full-time demand. I felt abused, as if he'd stuck me with his chore. He needed to come home or hire help, and he did. It had just never occurred to him that I wouldn't enjoy the family dinner hour or be natural with it. So I had to tell him," stated one woman.

Some men assume that women would rather they keep out of the way. That's the same kind of myth as the one about keeping fathers out of the nursery. Others go to the opposite extreme. One stepmother reported: "I was an onlooker around here until I convinced Judd to let me take some part in things. He said that he was so tempted just to hand his son over to me after being the only parent for so long. He had to learn to share the joy and the burden—to let me in." A stepmother must make certain that their two minds meet.

YOURS AND HIS

When stepchildren and parents live together, a marriage is not only the making of a couple but also of a community. Even mothers who bring their own children to the marriage are surprised to find that family structure as they once knew of it no longer applies. "You must be prepared to go into a less structured life and household. It takes a very long time for bonds to develop," said Kay, a mother of three who married a father of five.

When two sets of stepchildren are brought together by a marriage, a husband who is an active parent is enormously helpful, if not downright essential. Kay's husband stayed closely involved in the family scene. She stated, "He would sit up with a sick child, take his to the dentist, handle his children's problems. We tried to help each other, but we each had our hands full with our own. He ran his, and I ran mine. Both sets respected us as authorities. I think if we hadn't been sort of loose about the way things went around the house, we couldn't have made it. We went into a family situation that was unlike any family any of us had ever known. I quickly had to accept that I liked some of his children better than others. Two of them were very hostile. One was a dream."

Because Kay herself had no sons, the "dream" stepson took her last name as a gesture of affection when he came of age. "Despite some frictions between us, especially between the older stepchildren and me, we became a happy gang, but it took a lot of flexibility." No single problem merited much attention for long. "Some days I just thought, He or she is mad at me today. I'm mad at him or her, too. But we didn't have time to focus on it, and maybe that's why it got better. We had to keep moving along."

Stepmothers who bring children of their own to a mixed family setup soon discover that they can't develop a bond with stepchildren like the one they share with their own offspring. Notions that both sets of children will combine to become one big happy family fall flat. Stepmothers who strive for it are more likely to feel tension—products of the pressure between them and their stepchildren. However, natural mothers do have an advantage over childless women who become custodial stepmothers. They already have experience and confidence in their parenting abilities. Also, a stepmother with children is usually easier on herself. She doesn't need to prove her maternity to herself, and she is usually more likely to settle for becoming her stepchildren's friend.

When two families join under one roof, money can make a

big difference in the quality of life. It can buy household space, housekeeping help, baby-sitters, and vacation opportunities for the family of the marriage partners. Another big help is the acceptance of basic differences. "We live together, but that doesn't mean we're alike. My kids are more success-oriented and his children are more social. You don't homogenize," said a custodial stepmother. All that is true about stepmothering in general is accentuated in mixed families, as though each steprelationship is an exponent for strain and complications.

Holidays are typically times at which these families are stretched to the limit. Somebody's children, maybe all of them, always have to visit the other parent. If remarried partners want everyone to gather together, chances are they'll be disappointed. "We learned to take the good times when we were all together whenever they came, but they didn't usually come on holidays. Everyone was just too bugged with family responsibility over the holidays," one stepmother stated. Parents who celebrate holidays and special occasions with their stepchildren when their own children are off visiting their other natural parent often resent the situation. Yet romanticizing a family ideal, veteran stepmothers repeatedly warn, is a gross mistake. "Everyone has got to have enough space to breathe. If someone is putting pressure on kids to be here so that everyone can be together, they may learn to hate being all together. If, on the other hand, home is their haven, a place where they can relax from outside demands, then being together isn't so bad," a stepmother observed.

Relationships between two sets of children are invariably difficult and also require a couple's attention. Children in mixed households must make large adjustments in their lifestyles— another reason stepmothers are advised to be patient and take emotional reactions, especially territorial ones, into account. "All my daughter could think of when my stepdaughter planned to move in was that she was going to have to share her bathroom with her. She became obsessed by it. My biggest concern was that my stepchild would not disrupt my children's happiness."

After this stepmother shared her concerns with her husband, he raised the bathroom issue with his daughter so that she would be aware of the anxiety it was creating. The two stepsisters were required to share a bathroom, but peace was maintained, because the parents conspired to enforce tidiness and equal time in order to make certain the arrangement worked. The stepmother bought each girl a set of different-colored towels and added a new towel rack so that each would have her own. (Anybody audacious enough to wonder aloud what the big deal over a bathroom is all about had better not even try remarriage under one roof.)

Room-sharing is a common problem in mixed stepfamilies. A stepmother who moved into her husband's house with her daughter told how her mostly absent twenty-one-year-old step-daughter refused to have her new stepsister occupy her room. There is no all-purpose solution to these territorial disputes, except that parents must be united in their judgment and be ready to enforce their rules. Creativity helps. An imaginative solution that worked for a couple whose partners both brought college-age and at-home children to their marriage was that at-home children, including those who did not originally occupy the house, would have a room. The others had to share during their visits. "It also meant that they had to get acquainted," said the stepmother, who had that partly in mind when the rules about room arrangements were established. The parents cush-ioned the transition for the original room occupants by remodeling and reapportioning bedroom space more democratically, which is definitely helpful when you can afford it.

Stepchildren are also often troubled by the sexuality in their new household. "It's tough for them. The kids may be uneasy with sex anyway, and if the house is alive with sexuality, they sense it. Adolescents find this very disturbing," states Clifford Sager. He offers some special advice to remarried partners. "Don't smooch in front of kids or display a lot of intimacy until they're better accustomed to your living together and sharing a home." Time helps to remedy many of the initial adjustments to living under one roof.

As stepchildren are anxious about the stepmother who enters their midst, so do stepmothers feel equally uncertain about stepchildren who join their established households. "My stepdaughter lives so differently from us and my children that I insisted we have some counseling before she moved in," said one stepmother. "I told her it wasn't that I didn't want her, but I saw problems and I thought we were all going to need some help." Her husband reluctantly agreed to his wife's terms, since his daughter had a record of disciplinary and behavior problems. While the stepmother's daughter attends college classes every morning, her stepdaughter sleeps regularly until noon. Yet when the stepmother suggested it would be her stepdaughter's responsibility to fix supper and pull her weight around the house, her husband accused his wife of being unfair—of expecting work from his child that was not demanded of her own.

"I could see we were in for trouble. I felt I owed my husband the right to take in his own child, but only if she made an effort to fit in and if he would be equally involved in the process and adjustment," the stepmother stated. It was a sticky problem, but counseling helped. "I feel that she and I have a pact," said the stepmother after several counseling sessions. "I don't try to be her mother or to change her in any way, but she must accept the fact that I'm head of this house. Here she must conform to our household rules, dress properly when we go out together, and not introduce my child to drugs or other things she does that I don't want my child doing."

Surprisingly, the child who reacted with concern when the stepmother set forth her requirements was her own daughter. "She thought I was being mean. 'Mommy,' she said, 'you can't let her think you don't want her.' She identified with my step-daughter entirely. It was difficult all around, but now I think my stepdaughter is glad we dealt with her coming as a real event. There's been no ugliness, no testing, no surprises."

NEGOTIATION

Parents often resort to the family meeting to set policy and solve problems in large stepfamilies. The meeting itself, an arena for discussion with all family members, is widely considered a good idea—as long as it's not a democracy. "It's a mistake if the kids take over and run the show at family meetings. The meetings shouldn't be democratic. We advise the executive system, in which the adults are the executive committee, clearly above the others, or else it doesn't work," says Thomas Seibt. In one large mixed stepfamily, the stepmother, Marge, grew understandably unhappy when her stepchildren refused to accept the changes she proposed for the house. "Their mother was dead, and they wanted things left as they were," she explained. Meanwhile their relationship declined from warm through superficially polite to downright unfriendly. "Every change I made, they resented.

They even wanted the big old family portrait to stay up in the dining room. Of course, I didn't. I thought of it as my dining room now."

Though Marge could understand their attachment to photos and other mementos of their past family, she became resentful and angry when they tried to prevent her from putting a television set in the kitchen. "They said it was a tacky idea and that there hadn't been one there before," Marge reported. Her twenty-year-old stepson also began reprimanding her for her housekeeping habits. When he instructed her to put her dish in the dishwasher instead of setting it in the sink, she exploded. "The audacity of a twenty-year-old telling me where to put my dirty dish made me furious," she said.

Part of her problem, a psychologist pointed out to her, was that she reacted as hostilely to her stepchildren's comments and attitudes as she would have to an adult's. "I let them intimidate me. I should have just ignored them or put them in their place. Instead, I treated them as equals," she stated.

There is a strong argument for a new couple to set up house-keeping in a new location, but it is not always possible. Interest rates, comfortable old mortgages, space, and practical assets of a former home may make it impossible or imprudent to leave. Consequently, the conflict between a stepmother and her stepchildren may become territorial. She and her husband must draw the line. Marge felt her husband acted as an arbitrator of these conflicts but not as her partner. "He just didn't support me enough. He counted on me to understand. We knew it would be hard but not this hard," she said.

The psychologist who listened to her story spotted several stepfamily syndromes. First, she and her husband had not asserted their primacy as an "executive committee." In addition, the children's passionate defense of every household detail indicated that they had not finished grieving for their dead mother. Family counseling, which Marge eventually sought, was strongly recommended and made good sense. No one person should have expected to unravel, understand, or remedy the series of problems and emotional currents at work within Marge's new family. Her feelings of estrangement worsened when her stepdaughters refused to allow her daughter to move into the room that one of them, over twenty-one, occupied part-time. Though both sides probably dreamed of killing each other, her husband would not allow his children or her to say a disparaging word about the other. The pretense of civility while hostility teemed underneath made everyone feel that an explosion was likely to occur at any moment.

"Meeting this man was the best thing that ever happened to me, but parenting demands in this family situation are a real bitch," Marge asserted. When she began to see a therapist, she was angry. "It was their problem, but I was the one who had to go looking for help. I felt that they'd dragged my life down with their problems. I felt strongly that my husband and the children should seek help, too."

Psychologists and family counselors maintain that working with one or several family members can have a real impact on stepfamily problems, but therapy doesn't necessarily have to include everyone. In Marge's case, a psychologist first advised that she and her husband demonstrate that they were a "strong team." He said that they should work on the marriage and then on the family.

In general, professionals advise stepmothers not to be overly accommodating to mixed households. "All interpersonal relationships are expressed in terms of superficialities," states psychologist Margaret Doren. There is a symbolic importance to toothpaste and portraits and televisions or they wouldn't matter to us all so much. Thomas Seibt often tells stepmothers to set superficial limits on how far they will go to please stepchildren. "One woman's problem was keeping things for herself in the refrigerator. Her stepchildren took everything she bought. I told her she needed to start taking care of herself and she had better start somewhere. So she bought a carton of Cokes and announced that they were her Cokes and that she expected the children to keep away from them. It sounds small, but it was a start. She asserted a limit." Marge should put a television in her kitchen.

While it's essential to set limits and make clear to custodial stepchildren that you're the boss in your house, professionals and veteran stepmothers caution against squabbles or serious arguments between stepmothers and children. Avoid confrontations. Although quarrels and hostilities are common enough between parents and natural children, the parties have a relationship and a history that enable them to bounce back from hostility and other disciplinary showdowns. A stepmother and her stepchild, at least at the start of their relationship, do not. Harsh words can wound, and anger can anchor itself permanently in the psyche and the heart. Nobody needs bad feelings to linger on in a new family relationship.

A stepmother and child will never share the biological relationship that permits flesh-and-blood family members to rebound after disagreements and mend their fences, but if they share a life together, they are likely to create an affectionate tie that can eventually withstand some discord. "After the first year, I quit being jealous that somebody else was Charlotte's real mother," stated the custodial stepmother of an eight-year-old. "I know they share a genetic link, but I'm sharing Charlotte's day-to-day life, and our relationship is now based on what that means to us." It is usually the stepmother who ices the birthday cake, nurses the child with chicken pox, and accepts the May Day basket from school. The differences between custodial-stepmother and natural-mother relationships are similar to the differences between best friends and sisters. Sisters, like natural mothers and children, have an undeniable kinship, but best friends, who share so much of life together, too, are also bound closely. Their relationships spring from shared experiences, and their friendships may indeed be closer than some sisterly ties. Sisters and friends love each other in different ways, and the same goes for children and their mothers and stepmothers. A real mother's affection and behavior determine the affection a child develops for her, too. Though their link is constant, degrees of love and affection are also earned. But a stepmother should not expect a child to be objective about a mother, even a bad one. "Children respond differently to their biological parents. They feel defensive toward them. An attack on their parents is taken personally, so it's better not to criticize their mother or father," advises Lillian Messinger.

JOINT CUSTODY

Joint custody, though widely considered good for children because it helps them maintain relationships with both parents, often compounds the problem of stepmothers. Stepmothers are neither fish nor fowl, neither custodial nor noncustodial; and they have the handicaps of both. "They're here, but they're not really under my jurisdiction. Half the time I have all of the demands but none of the power," said a stepmother whose stepsons live with her every other week. She and her husband set aside and decorated a room for them, and when they are in res-idence (one almost slips and says *visit*), they figure into family plans and schedules. Stepmothers with such arrangements sim-ply must look on the bright side. Full-custody stepmothers would envy their child-free spell. Noncustodial women see the advantages in having routine family time.

Professionals offer another word of caution to custodial step-mothers. The task before them, that of uniting a new family under the same roof, often seems so great that many women approach it as a full-time job. Yet the woman who addresses her-self to it full-time is usually unhappy. As we've discussed, progress in the unpredictable realm of family relationships comes at its own pace. The woman who tries one plan after another and needs immediate tangible results to give her a sense of purpose and accomplishment in her new role is bound to be disconso-late. "In the cases we see, it's easier when both adults are work-ing, because the women don't expect so much, and they're less intense," states Clifford Sager.

Some stepmothers feel they have to devote themselves to stepmothering in order to whip their problems, but they're wrong. A new custodial stepmother who took a six-month leave from a satisfying job "to get everything in order at home" quickly became miserable. "I couldn't force anything to happen any faster than if I wasn't at home. Rather than have my work to concentrate on, all I did was think about our family, which I couldn't control anyway. I felt like a total failure. It was awful," she said. A stepmother of five young children believes that she successfully weathered the first two years of her marriage because she spent four days a week away from home during the summer months, finishing her graduate education. "I could get away from the stress and the personalities. I didn't run the risk of losing myself in it, of becoming obsessed," she asserted. And a third woman—who left her nursing career to care for four young stepchildren—doesn't regret the decision but said that she expected something in return that she never received. "When I took them over, I thought they would be like my children. Now I realize that they're not. They're still my stepchildren, and I put a terrible burden on them to make up to me for what I gave up when I left nursing. I felt I had to stay home and take care of them. I'd do it again, but I wouldn't expect so much."

Living with stepchildren is a real reach for women with and without their own children. "There are just things in my stepchildren's personalities and reactions that I have no control over," stated a stepmother, who added, "The degree of our differences probably wouldn't have surfaced if we didn't live together."

If you don't expect your stepchildren to take on your style or image, you probably won't be disappointed. The Visher counseling team suggests getting to know custodial stepchildren as you would any new roommates. Go to lunch together, perhaps enjoy a common sport. A shared family suggests built-in bonds, but stepmothers and stepchildren have to *build* them for themselves. "There's a lot a stepmother has to swallow in these situations," states Lillian Messinger, who recommends realism all the way. "Talk about instant love and loving them like your own is all a lot of hot air. Your goal should be to make a home for those kids, or to make a home for two families. Take it from there and establish your relationship around the positives."

19

Stepchildren with Problems

ew long-term studies on divorce report that
children of divorce suffer depression, learning
difficulties, and other psychological problems
more frequently than those of intact families. So
stepmothers shouldn't be surprised to discover
that stepchildren are often more troubled or
complicated than other children. That's a given.
Stepchildren, more often than not, have problems.

Long before I became familiar with stepmothering firsthand, I worked in an office with
a woman whose stepson wreaked havoc on her
home life. She arrived at work haggard-looking
on the morning after she and her husband had

gone to bail him out of police custody at 3:00 A.M. Then he made off with some family money. His misconduct touched her life incessantly. "We get along fine. He's just a bad kid," I heard her describe him. Believing that did not excuse her from becoming involved or make her dilemma any less difficult. He was her problem less than he was her husband's, but he was a negative presence in her life just the same.

Take stepchildren who are juvenile delinquents or car thieves. Their stepmothers may be relieved not to be the focus of their stepchildren's trouble, but a troublesome child touches their lives just the same. A caring and committed wife is unlikely to evade these problems by declaring them a nuisance and brushing them aside.

When dealing with problem children whom you, in fact, regard negatively, it's best to remember your place. The step-mother who rushes in and assumes the burden of a problem child as her own does everyone an injustice. She does not have the emotional commitment to strengthen her against the frustrations and responsibilities. And by putting herself deeper into emotional debt than she is ever likely to be repaid, she also reduces her chances of having a satisfying relationship with the child. To be concerned yet one step removed is a better position from which to support her husband through his parental strains.

A stepmother who used to wring her hands over her inability to reform a truant stepchild finally concluded, "If he goes to rack and ruin, I will help my husband pick up the pieces, but my involvement was useless. It created more problems than it solved." Psychologists applaud her sentiments. "You have to draw a line and stick to it about how deeply you're going to get involved in negative problems. Weigh whether your involvement helps or just makes you feel good," states Thomas Seibt. No matter what tack you decide to take, you must plot your behavior carefully.

With the conscious setting of boundaries and limitation of your involvement, you also need to guard against the opposite extremes. Becoming too detached, denouncing a stepchild as a "bad kid," or delivering a litany of his or her worthlessness will only set back your cause and alienate your husband. Keeping a step removed doesn't mean attacking a child's character. A natural parent must not be denied his connection, or have the worth of his efforts questioned, toward even the most difficult stepchild.

There are some general categories of serious-problem stepchildren that are more off-putting and alienating than others. An Electra complex is frequently described. A daughter, anywhere from adolescence to middle age, is excessively attached to her father. She feels possessive and makes her stepmother's life miserable, sometimes with tactics right out of soap operas. This child's intent, conscious or not, is to break up a marriage. It requires careful handling. You should withdraw to an emotional vantage point above the level of such a stepdaughter's manipulations. Try to spare yourself anguish and to help your husband foster his child's mental health.

One stepmother tells of a twenty-three-year-old stepdaughter who tried to upstage her at her own wedding. First the stepdaughter arrived in a white dress more suited to a bride than to the daughter of the groom. Then, as the wedding toasts began in the garden, she ran sobbing—theatrically, at the top of her lungs—into the house. A year later she still accuses her stepmother of everything from rudeness to gold-digging. "If I'm rushing to the bathroom and briskly say 'hi' as I pass her, she tells her father I snubbed her. She wants to cause trouble," the stepmother said. Holidays and other special occasions are the worst. The daughter suggests that her stepmother not spend the holidays with the family. When the daughter threw a birthday party for her brother, she suggested that her stepmother not attend—she said she would "ruin it for him." Wise to his daughter's motivations by then, the father refused to attend any gathering without his wife.

A psychologist counseled one earnest couple who felt divided because of a stepchild's refusal to visit her father in his home or in the company of his new wife. Children who ask you and their father to split up in order to accommodate their presence don't do so innocently. In a while the father reasoned that his daughter "just couldn't cope," and he believed her conduct was unintentional. The stepmother took it personally and saw it was an insult. Their counselor advised: "The child may be having trouble coping, but children who make these demands know exactly what they're doing. It gives them a sense of power."

The professional suggested several courses of action for the unhappy couple. First, the child should not be forced to do anything. Then she recommended that the father confront his child with her refusal to visit them together and let her know that he and his wife regarded it negatively. "Don't overlook or excuse bad behavior" was her advice. "A parent can be loving and still tell a child he won't agree to his or her terms. Let the choice become the child's." A stepmother must be able to accept that as well and not require more than a child is ready to give in order to satisfy her wounded pride or ego.

Learning to live with these imperfections makes the whole

difference in a stepmother's experience. Wrestling and raving against the way relations are, versus the way you'd like them to be, are as futile as banging your fist against a locked door. All you're likely to get out of it in the end are bruises.

Problem stepchildren aren't always malevolent. In one case a stepmother felt totally unequipped to deal with her thirteen-year-old retarded stepchild. "When I married Cliff, I knew that his daughter was retarded, but I had no idea of what being her stepmother would require." The problems included the physical demands of feeding, changing, bathing, and otherwise caring for the child. "Her mother is completely unable to discuss her and couldn't help me out. My husband was also at a loss. He had trouble coping with his guilt and anxiety over her," the stepmother stated.

The stepmother finally sought help from a doctor in a community hospital. "When Janie started menstruating, she was a mess. I couldn't believe it fell to me to handle all this, but it did. My husband was having trouble. I was having trouble. Thank goodness I had the sense to look for help." A nurse's aide was hired to help out part-time during her stepdaughter's visits, and the stepmother, a musician, adopted another self-help technique. "I admit it. I always schedule a lesson the weekends we have her so that I get some relief."

If you have acquired a stepchild who is a real problem, simply a bad egg, admit it to yourself. Otherwise, trying against the odds to reform such a child or taking his or her behavior personally will only make you miserable and endanger your marriage.

A stepmother should never declare outright dislike for a child, because children change and mature, and so do stepmothers. Yet it is permissible not to like a troublesome or unpleasant youngster. You should treat him honorably and politely—out of respect to your husband—but you don't have to lose any sleep over improving him or your relationship with him.

These relationships can and do change, but the factors that bring about the changes are usually outside a stepmother's control. When Betsy became a custodial stepmother of four children, she got along well with three, but the oldest, a boy, was a trial. "Thank goodness he went to boarding school, or I probably would have divorced his father. My stepson was very attached to his mother, and he tried to make my life difficult. He was also a snob, and he made it clear that he didn't think I was good enough for his father or him. But the worst thing he did was make fun of me to our friends and to the other children. He was tirelessly courteous to my face, but I always heard from the other kids that he ran me down behind my back and tried to make them dislike me. He put them up to mischief, dared them to embarrass me in public, saying something disparaging about what I was wearing or saying. It made me furious, and it hurt terribly," she said. Many years later, after his father's death, the stepson changed his attitude toward her. She observed, "He seems to have mellowed in almost every way. He frequently invites me to join his family for dinner, and he even remembers my birthday."

His turnabout became most evident when he told his younger brother, who conveyed the sentiment to their stepmother, that he was sorry about how he'd treated her. One reason behind the change was his own marital situation. Newly married to a woman who has become the stepmother to his three children, he now sees things differently.

Betsy smiled and said, "I can't really ever love him—he spoiled that. But it's past, and we're no longer enemies. I feel relieved. It was so hard for so long, and I never expected things would turn out like this."

Sometimes a stepmother may have to play amateur psychologist to sort out smaller problems with a difficult stepchild. It didn't take one woman long to spot the problem when her visiting stepdaughter invariably took something of her daughter's every time she visited. The things she stole were just little things like baseball caps, hairbrushes, and magazines, but the stepmother began to see a pattern. She also diagnosed the bigger problem. "My stepdaughter wanted the love and the role in the family that our daughter occupied." So she and her husband sat down with her and talked about it. They made it clear that taking things from her stepsibling was not acceptable, but most important, they aired her anxiety and adopted measures to make her feel better loved. "Just addressing the problem, letting her know we saw what was going on and cared about how she was feeling, seemed to help," said the stepmother. She began religiously inviting her stepdaughter to dinners and other occasions at their house. She also bought her some of the small accessory items like those she had swiped from her stepsister and gave them to her as casual presents, remarking offhandedly, "When I saw these I thought you might like them." Her husband doubled his efforts to be in touch and have time alone with his daughter. The thefts stopped.

20

Problem Stepchildren

Once upon a time there was a lovely woman, kind and good, who married her true love, a man with children. Because she loved her husband so, she was a wonderful stepmother to her stepchildren. She baked them cookies, made up their beds with fresh sheets, bought their Christmas presents, and always mailed their birthday cards on time. But her wicked stepchildren tried at every turn to make her miserable. The wicked stepdaughter, covered with warts and pimples, was so jealous of the fair new woman whom her father loved that she tried to poison the chocolates she gave her on Stepmother's Day. The wicked stepson backed his father's new car into a tree and told the father that his new wife had done it. Both stepchildren spit out her macaroni and cheese and left towels all over the bathroom floor when they visited. In their father's presence, these wicked children rallied around their stepmother with false cheer, but when he left, they cackled and hissed. "We will never love you," they screeched. "You don't belong. We'll ruin your marriage. " At which point, Lovely Stepmother, sick and tired of them, ate them up. Her husband understood.

There are two kinds of problem stepchildren: the ones you don't like and the ones who don't like you or at least have trouble warming to you. Usually, both a stepmother and her stepchildren adapt with time and learn to solve most of their problems. Yet sometimes a stepchild becomes a constant problem, frozen in a bad disposition and unresponsive. If a stepmother doesn't have a firm grip on herself, then anxiety attacks, marital discord, hives, and all other sorts of torment can result.

One woman was medically tested for the cause of an allergic reaction she developed at her family's vacation house where her stepchildren gathered together. The dogs, pillows, insulation, and shingles were all suspected as causes. She underwent many tests, but her ailment was not diagnosed. When she had the same reaction within hours of her problematic adult stepson's arrival in her city home years later, she thought she had solved the mystery. "I was allergic to him. I'm sure of it," she said.

The stepchild whose problems are caused by stepfamily circumstances, or who creates problems in stepmother-stepchild relations, is a common occurrence. That problem child, within the context of stepfamily relations, is one who refuses to respond or adapt to some semblance of normal stepmother and child relations. There are seeds of such subversive behavior in all stepchildren as they learn to reckon with a stepmother.

The symptoms are nearly universal. Stepmothers familiar with them will recognize them immediately. One is averted eyes, a refusal to make eye contact. Another is an unwillingness to say hello or goodbye. Variations of this include talking around you and avoiding acknowledgment of your presence. Of course, there are the ploys usually associated with food: "Mommy makes it better" or "I can't eat this." Most of these are simple signals to a stepmother that a stepchild hasn't yet accepted her presence. With increased familiarity, they usually pass. They're annoying, yes; they can even make grown women cry. But they're not devastating, and they shouldn't be allowed to ruin occasions or poison relationships, the way that real, hard-core problem stepchildren sometimes do.

Stepchildren can—and often do—demonstrate rapid and sharp personality changes. One moment you're both having a great time. You sigh with relief and conclude that there's hope for your relationship. Then wham! A chill settles in. What did you do? You wonder, What went wrong? Chances are your stepchild was beginning to like you. "The minute a kid withdraws or becomes hostile, a stepmother's next thought should be that the child is feeling guilty about his mother," states Clifford Sager, who explains that hostile behavior often follows on the heels of fun and affection—those pleasant spells a stepmother might call breakthroughs. He advises stepmothers to call attention to the shift in mood. "Gently ask a child if he's angry or feeling guilty because he's had fun or kind of likes you. The answer you get is less important than guiding him to understand the mixed emotions he's having."

YOU DON'T LIKE THEM

Even Daddy's darling and Granny's favorite, those family charmers, can leave a stepmother cold or treat her abysmally. For one of any of a number of reasons, a stepmother may find that she simply doesn't like her stepchild. "Let me put it this way—if my stepdaughter, Angela, and I were contemporaries, we wouldn't be friends," said a custodial stepmother who feels that she and her stepdaughter are different in every way. Another stepmother admitted, "My husband has two sons. One I enjoy a lot, but I don't like or respect the older one. He's lazy, manipulative, unhelpful, and rude to his father and the rest of us. If he were a stranger, I'd have nothing to do with him. Physically he also repulses me. I have to be careful not to recoil if he touches me."

Sometimes the differences between a woman and her stepchild don't constitute such strong aversion, but the differences between two totally different upbringings and styles can create a gulf between them anyhow. One stepmother said, "I think my stepdaughter is a spoiled brat. She's been indulged and pampered until her whole orientation to life is light-years from mine. If she gets a cold, she goes to bed for a week. I believe you keep going, trying to overcome setbacks."

Families make strange bedfellows, and a stepmother must vigilantly try to weed her prejudices and vulnerabilities out of her likes and dislikes of a stepchild. She cannot allow them to obscure her view or acquaintance with these new family members. In this regard, families are no different from other outside relationships. You wouldn't refuse to do business with a client or be cordial to a neighbor because of differences in your taste or background. The same goes for stepchildren.

It may seem contradictory to say that you must keep your distance in these new relationships, but it's true. You mustn't let your personal considerations determine your estimate of your stepchildren. For instance, it is clearly unfair to tag a stepchild as a spendthrift simply because money is tight in your home. These kinds of judgments are always tempting to a stepmother. It's easy to see how her likes and dislikes, coupled with the typical expectations of a loving relationship, can get interconnected in a woman's mind and drive her crazy. The combination is impossible, so those unrealistic expectations for loving have to go, and tolerance should be the order of the day.

All of us live and work among people with whom we feel very little kinship, but when such individuals turn up in our own family, we stepmothers are sometimes aghast and panicky. "That's why we spend so much time telling remarried partners that it's okay not to love their stepchildren. It takes the pressure off," states Thomas Seibt.

"I love my husband and our life, but I barely like my stepdaughter, Lucy. But it doesn't haunt me anymore that I feel that way. I had no say in her formative upbringing, and by my standards she's not a nice or interesting child. Who knows—I might feel that way about my best friend's kid, too. If Lucy disappeared from our life tomorrow, I'd hardly miss her," said a stepmother. But she has not shifted her attitude into the extremes of resentment or hate, and she also has the good sense not to decry her stepchild to her husband. Her outlook is truly pragmatic. "My husband probably thinks I care more for Lucy than I do. There's no sense dragging him through my negative feelings as long as they're not a problem for us. Itemizing my dislikes to him wouldn't change her, and he can obviously see that Lucy and I aren't best friends," she remarked. According to experts, her reaction is within the realm of acceptable stepfamily relations.

Stepmothers understandably have difficulty separating their feelings from their actions. It is perfectly fine to *feel* negative about a troublesome, difficult child, but your actions shouldn't reflect your dislike. You're not stuck with acting out your feelings, which may be less caring than you'd like to admit. "Feelings aren't right or wrong. They just are. But actions are different. It's the way you act that you can control," advises a psychologist. Stepmothers have to accept that they may not be able to control their feelings or manage them to be what they like. If you focus on altering your feelings, chances are you'll defeat yourself. Focus instead on controlling your behavior, and you probably won't feel so frustrated.

THEY DON'T LIKE YOU

As we already said, there are two kinds of problem stepchildren: the ones you don't like and the ones who don't like you. Unfortunately, the second group often ends up becoming part of the first group, too, in a progression that tortures many stepmothers.

Nothing hurts quite so much as approaching a child with high hopes, goodwill, and generosity—and being rebuffed. A relationship such as this quickly moves from a neutral quality to a negative one, a depressing outcome for the stepmother. It's fine—even correct, for what it's worth—to say that a woman should have been more cautious, and hoped for less, in these fragile relationships. But when they double back on a stepmother, causing her anger and resentment, it's a tough situation for her to dig her way out of. More good intentions or selfless gestures will just get her in deeper.

Her stepchild is obviously not going to bail her out and make good her emotional investment. Her position is a bit like that of a rejected suitor. She needs to lick her wounds, to rethink her position and options, rather than sink into bitterness or contempt. Don't plead or negotiate for anything your stepchild cannot give, The message is to back off. Never make an effort that risks all your pride; if it doesn't work out, your chances of a better relationship may be grievously harmed.

The trick for you is to keep your composure and cultivate some indifference to an offensive or unresponsive child. Don't cower in the face of rejection. Just make it clear, without being hostile, that your efforts at improving the relationship are over. "You can say as much," states Thomas Seibt. "Have it out. Just don't pressure." He suggests something like "I'd hoped we could get along or get to know each other better, but I can see you're not interested now." He feels it's all right to acknowledge these differences between you. You have to back off from the problem child, but you don't have to be a patsy. You or your husband should make a stepchild aware that there are consequences—your negative reaction, for one—for his actions. You cannot be expected or expect yourself to be a font of endless goodwill.

Unfortunately, stepmothers tend to punish themselves over their negative feelings toward a child, even one who has hurt them. "They shouldn't," says Seibt. "Of course, you'll be mad at someone who's rude or hurts you. There's nothing wrong with that." The trick is not to let negative feelings become an obsession. One stepmother declared such a war on her stepchildren that she installed a secret intercom in order to monitor their activities and to catch them in lies. Compulsively, she listened in. She had her proof, all right, but her obsession took its toll. She was a defeated and embittered person.

The problem child poses an extreme test for a stepmother in

terms of self-control and her ability to work around a trouble-some personality. While she must try to distance herself from the destructive effects of a problem child, she must be careful not to withdraw from the family, where she belongs. One woman fled—"like a total coward," she said—out of town without her husband to spend Thanksgiving with an old friend rather than brave the unpleasantness her stepdaughter threatened to cause if she stayed. Now she asserts, "That was wrong. When I got married, I expected to spend holidays with my family. From now on I stay. If she can't handle it, then we all don't have to be together. My husband has begun to see that, too." It's a mistake to flinch before relationships in which shows of confidence and marital unity carry so much weight.

A problem child must be accepted as part of a stepmother's new family. Nobody says she's got to be happy about it, but the ability to recognize and to accept what she cannot change can hardly be overemphasized.

Since you have to live with the same stepchild who offends or alienates you somewhere in your family picture, it helps to rebound from a rebuff with some self-respect and honesty. Let a disappointing stepchild know that you'd hoped for a better rela-tionship, but that you won't stick your neck out again without good cause. "It's a mistake not to confront negative actions, to go on as if this is normal behavior," notes Thomas Seibt. "Your stepchildren share and bear the consequences for your relation-ship as much as you do."

21

Outside Help

Hurt and humbled, many of us wisely look for help. Most people go to family counselors and psychologists, but there are also organizations like the Stepfamily Association of America in Baltimore, Maryland, and the Stepfamily Foundation in New York City, which offer support, advice, and substantial evidence that we are not alone in the universe with our anguish. But there is a hitch in seeking outside help. Family counselors and support groups will hear you out sympathetically, but they won't let you wallow for long in your problems. Ultimately, they expect you to be the architect of your recovery, and so you must be, even if you find the suggestion galling at the time.

While it's aggravating to hear that you're partly to blame for your anguish, it's reassuring to learn that changes within your control can have a positive influence. This isn't just the latest advertisement for the power of positive thinking. It's a recommendation for making sense out of a challenging and troublesome role in a way that may be impossible at the outset of stepmothering.

I don't mean to be a blanket advertisement or champion for psychologists and family counseling, but after talking with stepmothers, I came to the conclusion that counseling helps.

Invariably people benefited from counseling, and even those who formerly shunned the very idea of "seeing a shrink" or any other outside help say they profited from professional advice. The complexity of remarried family life often requires a disinterested third party with a professional understanding to help make sense out of the hash of personalities and emotional currents. "I can't tell you how wonderful it was finally to have someone I could be honest with. I could say that sometimes I hated my stepson, and she understood. She also had ideas for changing things. I grew less defensive and more tolerant of my stepson's side of things when I heard her say that mine were normal reactions," was one stepmother's description.

Counseling does not mean a lengthy commitment to weekly visits or psychoanalysis, as some women fear at first. Stepmothers usually visit a counselor from a few weeks to a few months, as long as it takes them to feel relieved and perhaps to apply some new principles at home. Some go back to a therapist again only when the going gets tough or they feel in need of new advice and a boost. Five visits are the norm.

"Until I got some help, I felt as if I was carrying around my husband's concerns, my two stepdaughters', my own, even my husband's ex-wife's. I took it all to heart, and it was too much for me. I sat across from the therapist with a box of Kleenexes in my lap and cried throughout most of the first session. I was so relieved to finally have someone to turn to. It was the first time I really became hopeful that things could get better," one stepmother said.

Another added, "It was just too much for me. I knew I wasn't crazy, but I knew that this marriage and family arrangement were more than I could deal with alone. I finally went because I thought I owed it to myself before I hired a divorce lawyer. I just didn't think I could take life the way it had become for me. I felt locked in, lost. But with help I began to see that I'd boxed myself in, too. I wanted perfection. I just couldn't accept the way things really were until somebody else pointed out my mistakes. Then I was even able to see my husband differently. I quit seeing him as the man who could solve everything for me. We were going to have to do it together."

Different kinds of problems require different kinds of outside help. If stepchildren have taken their toll on the marriage, then marital counseling may be necessary to set your relationship straight. Individual therapy can help if you feel the difficulty is largely a matter of your ability to cope. If a child is distraught and needs help, some counselors suggest that a whole family become involved. One woman sees her stepdaughter's psychologist once a month—as do her mother and father—to help correct a discipline problem rooted in the girl's adjustment to her parents' divorce and father's remarriage.

A psychologist or therapist obviously can't solve every grievance a stepmother has, but he or she usually can help you understand why you and others react as you do. A woman who reacts angrily to her husband's attention to his daughter, for instance, may need to examine why she feels so intensely angry. If his attentiveness is indeed excessive, she can try to help him see himself and understand his motivations, but if her hostility is rooted in her own personality, her family history, or her sense of inadequacy, she should get to the bottom of her emotions.

To any marriage, we all bring expectations and emotional patterns that are handed down to us from our parents. A woman who is furious with her own father for abandoning her mother, favoring her sister, or being insufficiently affectionate, may put unreasonable demands on her husband to satisfy her own insecurities. In less complicated family situations, it might not be essential to examine the inner landscape of your emotions and responses, but stepfamilies require special understanding from everyone in order to survive.

JOINT COUNSELING

When a marriage is the relationship that suffers most, as it often is, joint counseling can be enormously helpful. But for various reasons, husbands sometimes balk at seeking outside help. It helps if you understand *why* your husband is reluctant. Acknowledging problems in a new marriage may initially evoke the pain and memories of the first-marriage failure. It frightens a man to think that he may fail again, so he may refuse to see budding troubles this time around. But, in practice, once new-marriage difficulties are put in their proper perspective and seen as normal stresses in remarriages with children, reluctant husbands usually become receptive to counseling. A troubled stepmother may need (tactfully) to teach her husband that their experience is a joint problem, not a flaw in him that has returned to haunt him a second time around.

Men, still somewhat restrained by the cultural leftover of machismo, are usually more reluctant to seek help for personal and family problems than women are, but they usually can be persuaded to attend at least one session with a therapist. Thomas Seibt notes, "When you say, 'I'm having a really difficult time. Please come and help me learn to be happier,' someone who cares will almost always give it a try."

Family counselors say their first job is to teach couples that their tensions and turmoil are healthy, typical reactions in an extended family. Once both partners realize they are not unique, they are better able to let down their defenses and work toward solutions together. "It is so much better than being at logger-heads that both men and women feel relieved almost immediately," states Seibt, who also finds that second-marriage partners are extremely motivated to make their marriages work. Women married to divorced fathers may find in the end that their husband's commitment, patience, and determination match and eventually help to overcome the frustrations of stepfamily life. "They're in these marriages for much better reasons than they had in their first ones, and they really want them to work," Seibt says.

GROUPS

A support group serves the same function. Clifford Sager suggests that a stepmother try a support group before seeking therapy, because the discovery that other women have similar experiences can be greatly therapeutic in itself—and less expensive. "They're educational. A woman learns that others share her experiences and complaints, and she gets the chance to hear about their resolutions." If she then believes that she or her family would benefit from more personalized help, professionals can usually provide it. They can at least help her with her part in the stepfamily.

GOING ALONE

Being the only family member to enlist professional help often disgruntles a stepmother, but it can be effective nonetheless. "It wasn't my problem before I hooked up with all of them," one woman reasoned, "so why should *I* be going to the shrink?" Her reaction is understandable but not logical. There *are* reasons.

When stepfamily life gets out of hand, a change in approach from just one family member—the stepmother in this case—can have some impact. It alters the family chemistry. Even if it does not appreciably affect the whole situation, it can change her own experience. There is an element of personal advantage in it, too. If everyone in a family is floundering, it can be a big plus if the stepmother is the one who seeks help and advice and turns her therapy into a positive act.

Family life is not and should not be a power game, but it does not hurt a stepmother to give herself every advantage she can, to make her role more effective and her life more livable. She should realize that stepfamily life is often a game of roles and rivalries. As is true in most aspects of human relations, it helps to have a strong sense of yourself, your values, and your purpose totally aside from family definitions. This is especially true of stepmothering, a state of being that questions who you are and what you are about many times every day.

22

You

espite the limits of her role and experience, a stepmother is regularly the pivot point in a complex and unorthodox family arrangement. Without her there is a divorced man and his children. With her there is a marriage, a stepfamily, and a whole set of steprelations. Frictions, tensions, and complaints can become lodged in the crevices between the various conditions.

The centrality of her position is a shock to a stepmother. Her goal is to be able to function at the center of a family and to stay true to herself at the same time. Natural mothers are similarly challenged by the dual demands of marriage

220

and family life, but—and it's a big but—they have the security and inspiration of the biological tie to their children. In addition, the logistics of natural family life are much simpler than they are in stepfamilies. Juggling so many concerns may often seem like an unfair burden on you and your marriage. After all, your husband's first wife didn't have to rise to this test.

Frustration, anger, fatigue, even resentment are natural reactions for a stepmother. Being adult shouldn't mean being saintly or superhuman. It should mean being realistic and learning to weather adversity, but it doesn't mean being invulnerable to strains. Some days you clearly don't like your stepchildren, and you don't feel like being sensitive to someone else's feelings.

It's all right—even healthy—to feel that way. Professional texts on the subject of remarriage with stepchildren all mention the negative feelings and strain common to stepmothers. No stepmother should feel freakish for having spells in which she doesn't love her position or her stepchildren.

There is no cure-all for the maladies of stepmothering, no inoculations against problem children and vacation hassles, for instance. You're likely to catch this occupational disease. Yet there are methods to help you keep from languishing under its effects, and to moderate the worst symptoms—once you understand the nature of the illness.

Recognize that stepmothering is a long-term, ongoing, probably permanent affair. Though the majority of women interviewed for this book were still actively involved in coping with minor stepchildren, those who were not still experienced some confusions and problems in their stepmothering relations. The age of children may minimize the intensity and frequency of differences between a woman and her stepchildren, but just like parenting, stepparenting is forever.

One stepmother who barely knew her stepson when he was living at home with his mother now finds that the adult, whom she has come to know better, is a bit difficult to come to terms with. "He was a foreign individual to us both," she said. She shuddered when the California-reared son of her husband walked around barefoot in the snow outside her East Coast home. This year he brought his wife and child along on his annual visit. Every time his wife nursed the baby, he, a new evangelical Christian, prayed aloud. "It was trying for me to have all this going on. I saw a lot of humor in our contrasts, however. If I thought life was deadly serious, I'd never make it," she asserted. She finds a sense of humor a great asset when dealing with older stepchildren.

It also helps for a stepmother to put more energy into being a wife than into being a stepmother. To do otherwise would be to misplace emphasis on a most uncertain relationship. The time and effort that a woman puts into marriage are much more likely to yield rewards. Furthermore, that marital relationship is an essential reference point for stepmothering. First things first. It is better to strive to be part of a healthy couple working together to minimize the strains of steprelationships than to be the guiding light of "one big happy family." As we've seen, stepmothering doesn't necessarily enhance your life; some stepfamily relationships undeniably detract from a woman's happiness. That reality requires compensation.

A BREAK

Throughout this book, the message for the stepmother has been to trim her expectations for stepmothering and to chart her course with confidence. Still, even when things are going well, a stepmother needs a break. Psychic fatigue comes from the added strains of stepmothering. A stepmother has a distinct need for private time and space to assert her identity apart from the larger family.

Taking a break can be a small or a large matter. Sometimes it's as small as a long hot bath while everyone else plays Monopoly or as big as your suggestion that your husband go without you to parents' weekend this year. These pauses don't constitute a substantial change in a stepmother's lifestyle, but they can provide psychological relief and a respite against strain. If you're not borrowing against the time you and your husband need as a couple, try persuading your husband to be a bachelor at home for a week so that you can have a vacation alone or with an old chum. Do something that takes you away from stepfamily considerations. On a smaller scale, promise yourself a treat—a lunch date, movie, massage, new pair of shoes, whatever—as a reward for hostessing the annual summer family reunion at your house. These things may sound gimmicky, but they go a long way toward taking the grind out of stepmothering.

Backing off from the daily routine of stepmothering invariably causes some guilt feelings. Real mothers, more certain about their role, know that a break is essential, but there is no precedent for the emotional distance that a stepmother sometimes needs to put between herself and her stepfamily. At times she needs to dissociate herself from the needs of the family. Perhaps a stepmother should learn to think of backing off, or taking time out, as compensation for not having the final authority in her family relationships. Like the second-ranked officer in a corporation, she should leave some of the headaches and duties to the chairman while she takes a vacation.

One response to the confusion and ambiguity of stepmothering is overinvolvement, as if the answer is to immerse oneself in family life for identity and meaning. The result is usually disastrous, because a stepmother doesn't have a natural full-scale place in a stepfamily even if she has been the maternal head of her own household. An existing family cannot reshape her life the way that natural mothering might, A stepmother's ties and duties to her stepchildren are not based on the same basic drives that bind a child and motivate a parent. So she must content herself with touching her stepchild's life in different ways and places. It takes skill and effort.

The fact that you are not your stepchildren's mother should spare you hurt, rather than bring it your way. A family psychologist warns: "Don't let yourself be hurt by your generosity. Remind yourself that they're not your children. You can only provide input." The limitations of a stepmother's role can be a relief if she will recognize them.

One stepmother was intent on helping to provide her stepdaughter with the opportunity to study in Europe, as she had done. It had changed and enriched her life, and she wanted a similar experience for her stepdaughter. When given the choice, however, the girl chose not to go. At first, her stepmother reacted like a parent, distressed by a decision that she considered a mistake. She fashioned arguments for her stepdaughter's studying abroad before falling asleep at night, and she repeatedly discussed the subject with her husband. Then she came to her senses and stopped. She remembered that she had gone to Europe because it had been a driving ambition. Her own mother had shared and supported it. However, the stepmother realized that her stepdaughter did not share that particular ambition, and that was that. For her to struggle to persuade her to do something that she didn't want was ridiculous.

This stepmother is a realist, not a coward. She had made her case and lost. She recognized that if her stepdaughter had been her own child, she would have tried harder to bring the girl around to her way of thinking. But that's a parent's prerogative, not a stepmother's.

The realization combines both a sense of loss and of freedom: loss of influence and control and freedom from any risk to your investment as well. If the stepmother had been her parent, she would have taken her refusal more personally. Said a veteran stepmother, full of insight, "With stepchildren you are finishing somebody else's artwork. It is never going to look like the picture you would have painted if you had started from scratch."

A stepmother who reacts with deep emotion to the behavior of her stepchildren usually has invested too much of herself in them. One woman made a huge issue about her noncustodial stepson's eating habits. "He eats only junk at home," she complained. Determined to change his ways, she started a health food crusade when he was visiting. When the issue became a combustive family issue, she had to admit, "I was trying to say that I loved him like my own, and I couldn't admit he went home to a different mother. So I latched on to the food thing. It was the only area of his life I could control."

BACKING OFF

Being a stoic isn't the right approach either, but overinvolvement costs a stepmother her own emotional well-being and is ultimately detrimental to stepparenting relationships. The child of whom too much is expected invariably fails, and then he or she is likely to resent the standards of the test. Love isn't always the issue either. There can be obsessive overinvolvement without it.

Natalie was so distraught over her stepson's sloppy appearance and depressed behavior that they dominated her mood and conversation before and after his visits. "I felt total anxiety. I perspire and get flushed just talking about it. I wanted to straighten him out. I wanted my husband to change him. I wanted change, change, change." Any stepmother might have wanted the same thing, but when getting or not getting a certain result from a stepchild becomes an obsession, a stepmother has to pause and take stock. Natalie went to a psychologist who advised her to back away from her own frustrations. "She said that in areas like this where I was ineffective at getting change from reasonable suggestions, I should move back. I shouldn't ignore my stepson, but my job is to help my husband *manage* his parental role, not *create* it for him. If Skip doesn't heed my advice, then I should concern myself with him only insofar as he affects my life. I can ask him to wash up before dinner, for instance, but I can't ask him to change his life."

Obviously, a stepmother can offer help, and sometimes she can greatly affect a stepchild beyond the normal limits of their relationship. But if doing so is not natural to their relationship and becomes a one-sided struggle on her part, she should stop.

INFLUENCE

Stepmothers can contribute a great deal to those stepchildren who are receptive to their influence. This commonly overlooked fact ought to improve stepmothering's public image and boost our self-esteem. Each of us recalls some person—a teacher, family friend, or distant aunt—who made a sizable impression on our lives by the sheer strength of his or her personality and appeal. Sometimes the influence of those individuals can be greater than any prescribed role model's. That possibility is certainly open to stepmothers. However, a stepmother's highest goal should not necessarily be to have an impact on her stepchild. The main thing is to make a favorable acquaintance with him or her and to establish some ease in their relationship. Impact comes later. What she can offer—and what her stepchild can accept later—is a bonus.

Children of divorce who become stepchildren are fortunate to be able to add another caring adult to their family population. A stepmother doesn't have to apologize for being an extra person on the scene. Learning to live and to work with diverse personalities is a good skill for children to take into life. In addition, a stepmother may make more specific contributions simply by her presence. A career woman may offer a useful contrast to the nonworking mother, demonstrating a different kind of lifestyle to the stepchild. An artist can open up a new world for a child. The list is endless. Your example—quirks, kindness, temper, ambitions—has an impact of some sort on the lives you touch.

"I think Alice has gotten a lot from me. I've broadened her exposure to the world, that's all. Her family has money. I didn't. She's seen my work and accomplishments. She knows I went to city college and worked as a typist. She seems to respect these things, and I think she understands that life is something you can make happen *for* you, not *to* you. I feel happy about that," one stepmother said.

Ironically, another stepmother is the one who gives the motherly touches to her stepson's present life. "His mother is busy making a new life, dating and discovering herself, so I'm the one who sends brownies up to school and has long talks about life with him over Christmas break. I'm not his mother, and we both know that. But this way he gets the whole package one way or another," stated his stepmother.

Stepmothers usually don't give themselves credit for the contribution they make to their stepchildren. One important study shows that we invariably rate ourselves lower than our stepchildren would. Your stepchild is likely to think that you're doing well by them while you worry that you should be doing better.

REWARDS

What a stepmother receives from a stepchild in return is unpredictable. Stepmothering, like real parenting, is not based on the barter system. Affection has its own bursts and chills and growing spells. A stepmother must try to establish a place for herself outside a child's parental relationships, not as a rival to the parent.

Stepchildren, like the rest of us, must experience the impact of their parents on their psyches and lives. A stepmother is wise not to crowd them and to keep in mind that while children generally love their parents, they do not always like them. A stepchild may be freer to care for you on neutral emotional territory.

A thirty-three-year-old stepmother-to-be wondered aloud, "What will our relationship be when I'm old? Will my stepchildren come help me find a nursing home? Will they visit? Do they go in my will?" There are no clear-cut answers. Stepmothers and stepchildren have virtually no legal attachment unless a stepmother adopts them. They'll be in her will if she puts them in.

It is heartening to hear that for some stepmothers and their stepchildren their relationships are close and meaningful. "I'm closer to my stepdaughter than I am to my own two girls," noted a stepmother who is sixty-two years old. "We all lived together, and I had so many expectations for my girls. Sometimes those expectations caused problems. They're still dealing with those, but my stepdaughter and I are better friends. She's the one who helped me to see what was going on between me and my daughters. I love them more than my stepdaughter, but it's more difficult for us to get along together," she said.

Another woman has designated one of her stepdaughters in her will to become the legal guardian of her own young children if she and her husband should die at the same time. "I think that shows how much I think of her. I would entrust my dearest possessions to her. I don't feel this way about my other stepchildren, but my relationship to this girl is special," she stated.

MODERN TIMES

Modern stepmotherhood is gradually becoming a little more predictable. As stepmothers free themselves of the crippling stereotypes and disappointments, the kinds of relationships available to them become manifold. We are free to fashion our own kind of connections with our stepchildren and to apply the natural give-and-take of human relations. We can actually begin, on our own terms, to make sense of stepmothering. The likelihood for emerging from our predicaments, solving our problems, and alleviating stepfamily pressures on our lives is greater than ever before.

Your success depends a lot on your skill at adapting to and growing in your role. Maturity is a very popular buzzword among family professionals talking about assets for stepmotherhood. These professionals speak of maturity not as a grim posture of adulthood but as the emotional development that enables a woman to judge and respond to challenges and obstacles.

A sense of family may show up when you least expect it. One woman told of her surprise and gratitude when a stepdaughter with whom she had experienced many differences—and forged only a tentative peace—surprised her with an outburst of warmth and sympathy. "I ran into her when I was in tears over the death of my favorite uncle. She didn't say much. It was obvious I was very upset. Later in the day she called my office to see how I was and to say she was worried about me. She said she wanted me to know that she loved me." Such heartwarming times are probably not rooted so much in familial ties as they are in simple friendship. Perhaps that should be a stepmother's highest goal.

In another instance a woman's stepson kept in touch with her well after her marriage to his father ended. "I had been there for him a lot, when he had trouble in school, trouble at home. I was always the one waiting at the airport when he came to visit his father and me. He didn't forget it," his stepmother said. A child's response to a stepmother often has more to do with the personality of the child than the success or failure of the stepparent. A stepmother can only assure herself, as natural parents do, that she has fulfilled her duties, and then all she can do is hope for the best. She has more reason than natural parents to make sure that she keeps her self-image separate from the evident regard (or lack of it) in which a stepchild holds her. Too many things are too often against her for a stepchild's opinion to be a fair mirror of her concern or efforts.

It is extremely difficult to depersonalize stepmother relations, but sometimes a certain detachment is essential to protect yourself. Stepchildren who behave the worst are usually unsettled in their relations with their own mother and father. Their bad attitude toward a stepmother is rooted in those troubled relationships, and although a stepmother can't overlook it, she shouldn't take it too personally.

Stepmothering has its golden moments, too, and they are often as difficult to define as other aspects of stepmothering because they are feelings that do not fit neatly into any already established category. Stepmothering highs and tenderness are invariably based on a sense of success and fondness—shared. Emily Visher describes her own feelings in most clinical terms: "I get a warm feeling when I get a birthday card from my kids, but when I get a birthday card from one of my stepchildren, I get a warm feeling and something else inside. Our relationship is very special because we created it." A stepmother becomes aware of what it takes to develop a relationship and to keep it. That in itself is one of the most prized accomplishments in human relations. Nothing is taken for granted. We are forced by our circumstances to become aware of every aspect of our relationship.

Modern stepmothers are constantly showing the success that it is possible to achieve in the role, but the experience is usually a far cry from their original expectations. They learn to leave a lot of their theories and preconceptions by the wayside. Freed of excessive emotional reactions and unrealistic expectations, you, too, can move forward with a new ease and special knowledge of your new family terrain. What you bring along is equally important. Self-knowledge, flexibility, and a conscious determination to succeed in a new kind of family are all things to have with you when you venture into this always unpredictable relationship.

23
The Older Stepfamily

t's not the age of the stepmother but the duration of the stepfamily that makes the distinction between an older and a new stepfamily. A woman over forty can just as easily be a new stepmother and a thirty-five-year-old may already be a stepmother of half a dozen years or more. What matters is time and experience.

LEARNED DETACHMENT

As stepfamily professionals predict, and stepmothers discover, relationships stabilize between stepfamily members after three to five years. *But "stabilize" does not mean that a stepfamily becomes like a traditional family.* "The fact of life is that you are always a somewhat unwelcome person even if your stepchildren develop a fondness for you. Even if life wasn't as good with their mother, they liked it better that way," a stepmother of seventeen years concluded. She has learned to stay somewhat detached emotionally from her stepchildren. "Otherwise, you could spend your whole life fighting a losing battle," she said.

As I've talked with stepmothers in older stepfamilies I've learned that most of us are surprised by the way stepfamily issues remain constant. They may play out in different arenas and at different ages, but they don't go away entirely. The stepchild who had trouble adjusting to you as a teenager may seem to have gotten over the breakup of her traditional family and your entry to her life, but her marriage, the birth of a child, or even something as simple as your casual criticism can make the old issues flare up when you least expect them to. If you scratch beneath the calm surface of older stepfamily relationships, pain—real or remembered—is easy to unearth.

One stepmother's story embodies some of the truths in an older stepfamily. After years of relief from stepfamily stress or incidents, the stepmother was troubled when her stepdaughter turned up in clothing that seemed out of place—and out of character—at a fashionable family social occasion. During her teens her stepdaughter, a pretty girl, had taken a certain pride in her clothes and appearance. Fifteen years later, she was a successful college graduate, wife, and mother. Her stepmother interpreted her inappropriate dress and withdrawn manner as unhappiness or depression. Her husband also found his daughter's appearance and behavior worrisome, but he read less into it than his wife did.

The stepmother struggled with herself after the visit. She

worried that her interference would rock the boat and was likely to be misinterpreted by her stepdaughter as judgmental. On the other hand, she had begun to feel like the only family member who recognized her stepdaughter's distress. Finally, she decided to stop feeling like a stepfamily coward and prevailed upon her husband, who agreed that his daughter did not seem like herself, to talk to her.

What emerged during a tearful conversation among the three of them was that the stepdaughter still felt a great deal of pain about being the child of what she called "the failed marriage" rather than of her father's second marriage and family. She said she had felt like a second-class family member at the party, which had been an emotional affair for her. The stepmother was accused of being critical and holding her to too high a standard. Her concern was not appreciated.

In hindsight she noted that what made the difference between this and earlier difficult episodes in her stepfamily experience was her reaction to it. "I was disappointed, but I didn't let it make me miserable. I managed to stay a little bit removed," she said. Her stepdaughter's feelings are one of those things she is powerless to change. "You do your best and then you have to walk away. My stepdaughter is an adult now, I can't fix her life," she concluded.

OLD ISSUES REAPPEAR

The other lesson in the episode above is that old issues often reappear in disguise. The stepmother thought that her step-daughter's marriage, career transition, or the strains of having young children were reasons for her seeming unhappiness. "Instead, we were right back at square one—her parents' divorce

versus the family her father and I have together," said the stepmother. They have been over this ground before. "I think it's natural to feel the way my stepdaughter does, and I don't want to
see her in pain. I'd like to help. But the truth is that I can't. Her
father and I have been married a long time now. She has some
responsibility for helping herself," she said. To those without
stepchildren, such reactions might sound callous, but to stepmothers they are realizations important to survival and can make
the difference between a happy or horrible existence.

"I take great pleasure in the extended family but I no longer
have any fantasies about being one big, happy family. It's hard to
have a big, happy family," says a stepmother of sixteen years, who
remembers the shock of the first Christmas dinner she cooked
for three stepchildren who were disappointed that she had
changed the menu from what their mother used to serve. "My
fantasies are dispelled now. I cherish the lovely moments we have
together, but the bottom line is, if you're trying to be a perfect
stepmother, it's disastrous," she said. She exchanges a meaningful
glance with her husband each year at Christmas when her stepdaughter invariably finds a way to assert her sentiment that
something was better the way Mom did it. After sixteen years
her stepmother knows what to expect and how to react to it.

A ROLE OF HER OWN

Several things make a stepmother's life in an older stepfamily
easier. Her experience at handling stepfamily problems and a
shared history with her stepchildren both work to make stepfamily frictions seem less threatening than they did at the beginning of her marriage. In an older stepfamily tensions between a
stepmother and her stepchildren are more likely to feel like a

setback than a complete crisis. A stepmother is hopefully more secure in her marriage and more familiar with the personalities in her family, which also contribute to make later stepmothering easier. She has earned her place.

For another stepmother, her progression over the years to a genuine place in the family has given her a better perspective on its personalities and frailties. The different roles she filled during family drug counseling after her stepson's two drug overdoses, ten years apart, best exemplify the change. "The first time I was really just an onlooker, but the second time I considered myself a part of the family and someone who could try to affect some healing," she said.

CHANGING NEEDS

As the needs of stepchildren change, their relationship to a step-mother changes, too. A stepmother of twenty years reflects on how close she was to her stepson during his college years. She traveled to see his college football games and created family occasions with him and his father during the first few years he attended a nearby college. She welcomed the opportunity to earn a genuine role in her stepson's life and to prove that she was generous and caring. While his own mother adjusted to a different life and her own new marriage, her stepson needed and seemed to appreciate her affection and support. He brought his friends home to meet her and his father and frequently dropped by their house.

However, in recent years both his and her needs—and relationship—have changed. The stepmother's focus is on the children she and her husband have together, and her stepson, an adult, is occupied with his own life. He is an adult rather than

the needy teenager who came into her early marriage. If a stepmother can see these changes as evolutions rather than losses in
her relationships to her stepchildren, she will feel better about
them. "It's easy to feel bad until you admit that you've changed,
too," said one such stepmother. The same is true among biological mothers and children, but their underlying bonds hold
tighter through life's changing cycles.

Sometimes things change for the better. One stepmother had
a rockier start with one of her two stepchildren. Yet that
stepchild is someone she better relates to these days. After almost
twenty years in a shared constellation of family life, the two have
some things in common, especially some of the people they
both love. They've evolved a relationship based on common
interests that wasn't possible when the stepmother was the
father's new wife and wanted first and foremost to "get it right,"
and her stepdaughter was held hostage to her mother's resentments. The stepmother no longer interprets her low-key
approach as hostility, and the stepdaughter seems more accepting
of the differences between them. There is a warm and unforced
aspect to their relationship now that could not have been
achieved earlier. The stepdaughter is married, a professional, and
lives in a different city, but she and her father maintain a phone
and e-mail relationship that doesn't routinely include the stepmother. And everybody—including the stepmother—is comfortable with that. The resulting relationship feels honest and
natural.

THE PROBLEM WITH GOOD STEPMOTHERS

Another irony of stepmotherhood is what I call the "good stepmother syndrome." If a stepmother does good things for her

stepchild when the natural mother doesn't, she may not be appreciated because, ironically, it shows up the mother's failing, which is painful for a stepchild. A young mother of a newborn was troubled that her own mother had not managed to visit her and her baby though her in-laws, father, and stepmother had. Her stepmother brought gifts and words of assurance, but it was difficult for this new mother to feel appreciative. "It made me feel bad that it wasn't my mother," she explained later in a frank talk with her stepmother.

What is a stepmother to do? She should not be inhibited from doing for her stepchildren the things that come naturally to her, but she should not expect to be appreciated as she might in other relationships. Be aware of the complexity of these relationships, which grow ever more tangled as stepchildren grow older and more conscious themselves of the intricacy and resonance of stepfamily relationships and feelings. An eight-year-old stepchild may be just plain grateful to have a fun weekend with you, but an adult has more on his or her mind. It would be a mistake to expect to be appreciated on a plane that is reserved for real parents. "A stepmother can't be a Band-Aid for an adult," cautions a stepfamily therapist, who warns stepmothers that no matter how loving their relationship with a stepchild may be, if the natural mother is unreasonable, the child's frustrations usually get displaced onto the stepmother. "It's not fair, but it's the way it is," she cautions, "so don't get in too deep emotionally."

What you give or extend of yourself may be received and taken to heart by your stepchildren on some level, but acknowledging it can be painful or cause you to feel disloyal to them. As the stories above show, the result of a stepmother's actions may not be exactly what she intended. Yet she is not wrong to act, rather than withdraw, from stepfamily connections and involvement. She must, however, stay well enough anchored in an understanding of herself and her fellow family members not to be knocked off balance when things don't work out as she'd hoped.

HAPPY SURPRISES

"It's an illusion to think you can truly work everything out," says Teresa Adams, a leading family therapist and stepmother herself in New Orleans. "The effects of divorce and the creation of a stepfamily live on with adult stepchildren," she says. But Adams reports that there are often happy surprises for stepmothers later in stepfamily life. One of those is the spontaneous and open relationships that can be developed with stepgrandchilden. "Love blooms when the stepgrandchildren get to know you for who you really are—without the baggage of the past," she says and tells a story about her own five-year-old stepgrandson: " 'I need to tell you something,' he said. 'You know my mother? Well, she has a mother, and it's not you. You know what? She has a father, and it's your husband!' " The story delights her. "You have a natural affinity to your stepgrandchild and they also help connect you to their parents, who become far more compassionate once they appreciate that parenting is an arduous task." Stepchildren who marry and have their own families are often easier for stepmothers to enjoy, simply because they have moved on emotionally themselves.

After thirteen years of marriage one stepmother was amazed at the ease with which she and her husband's ex-wife and husband began spending a week at the same vacation resort every summer with her stepchildren and stepgrandchildren. "We do it so we can all be together with the kids, but it has been great for everybody. I feel that all parts of the family have managed to share these life cycles. It's been beneficial for the kids and I have to admit that I like how it ties us all together." Perhaps, she confessed with a rueful smile, she is still hostage to that big, happy family fantasy of early stepmotherhood, but at least her hopes are scaled by experience. The ease of these shared occasions would not have been possible when she and her husband first married. "I think my husband's ex-wife and I had to be sure that we were both decent people. It helped that she would say something flattering about me to her children that got back to me, and vice versa. I'd heard so much about her for so long from my stepchildren that I felt like I knew her anyway, so spending time around her felt natural."

Life events, such as weddings, are also the reward of older stepfamilies, not just the sweaty-palmed affairs they can be for younger stepfamilies. "There's the child whose laundry you've done and sent to camp, coming down the aisle, now the bride or groom, and it's wonderful to see," said a stepmother of three. She got better, she said, at handling stepfamily occasions with each successive wedding. In a younger stepfamily special events are more likely to be orchestrated by the natural parents and the stepmother sometimes feels like it's a struggle to find a niche for herself, but in the older stepfamily, a stepmother may find herself more central to the process. Then the trick is to know your place.

The stepmother above and her husband hosted each of her stepchildren's weddings in their home. They were successful, she thinks, in part because, "I never tried to usurp their mother's role or wanted to walk down the aisle first. You learn that the focus is the joy of the child having a festive time and not the pecking order."

Another reward for stepmothers in older stepfamilies is seeing the way children, siblings, and stepsiblings often bond together as adults. "The clan bonds from having been through so many things together and its members don't worry so much about who is from what side anymore," says a stepmother who was delighted that her children and stepchildren took part in each other's weddings. A family trip to a dude ranch that mixed the children of both spouses from their first marriages and their children together provided another occasion for fun and shared memories. "The boundaries are different and everyone has fun together. Fun is maybe more important to share in a stepfamily than love," said the stepmother.

POTENTIAL FOR PAIN

Despite the success of such family occasions and almost twenty-five years of stepfamily life, one stepmother learned firsthand that the potential for stepfamily pain is always lurking. Several years ago she experienced what the family refers to in almost hushed tones as the Chicken Pox Christmas. Traditionally all the children went to her husband's parents' house for the Christmas holiday. Some came for Christmas Eve, others for Christmas Day, but everyone made an appearance. That year the oldest stepson's three-year-old had chicken pox and her second stepson's wife was in the first trimester of pregnancy. The pregnant wife could not be exposed to the child with chicken pox, so all family members were required to shuttle in and out of the grandparents' house. The stepmother and her son ended up staying in a motel and her husband commuted between his adult children and her. "He tried to please everybody and ended up pleasing nobody," she recalled. No one wanted to be left out regardless of age and everyone felt left out by the exclusive circumstances. "It touched all the old wounds and vulnerabilities. It was a real reminder that you may think you've left all those problems behind, but events can always touch emotions that circle back and get you."

AGE HELPS

Events can always stir up old emotions and resentments on short notice in older stepfamilies, but the good news is that troubled times occur less frequently and cause less damage when a stepmother and her stepfamily have years of shared experience. A stepmother's age also helps. Says a stepmother of three, who recently turned forty, "In a marriage like ours with young children your lifestyle revolves around the kids. I wouldn't have understood that—or wanted to—when I was twenty, but at forty I do." She was just recently reminded that stepfamily life can be wildly unpredictable. Her husband's ex-wife, who has been estranged from her stepchildren for twelve years, returned this year expecting to normalize relationships with them. "When I was in my twenties I wouldn't have been able to deal with this," says the stepmother, "but now I just take things a day at a time. I know they'll get better and we'll get through it."

It may not be age as much as the experience that comes with it that is a stepmother's best teacher. The more experienced we are at life, the easier stepmothering gets. It's not just how you cope, but what you know, that helps to make the difference.

Resources

www.stepfamilies.com
This site provides support and positive advice about finding outside professional help and net-working with other stepparents.

www.stepfamilyinfo.org
Check here for nuts-and-bolt references aimed at finding solutions to problems.

www.stepfamily.net
Easy to read and access, this site provides a national directory of stepfamily counselors. Changing topics and questions go to the heart of the stepparenting experience.

www.stepmoms.net
This is a site with some attitude. You can vent in the chat room or find a stepmother pen pal.

www.stepmothers.org
This site is a branch of the Stepfamily Association of America focussed on stepmothers and aimed at promoting understanding through communication and support.

Index

family counseling. *See* counseling
family gatherings, 155–63
    ex-wives' inclusion at, 51–52
    funerals, 157
    graduations, 159–60
    holidays, 124, 127, 132–40, 189
    vacations, 123–31
    weddings, 158–60, 240
family law, 145, 150–51
family meetings, 192
financial issues, 141–54
    alimony, 66–67, 144, 146–47, 149, 151–53
    child support, 141–47, 149–53
    ex-wife's situation, 66–67, 144–53
    generosity's benefits and pitfalls, 142, 147–48
    inheritances, 64–65, 145, 228
    mixed stepfamilies and, 188–89
    post-divorce litigation, 150–51
    prenuptial agreements, 145
    stepchild's wedding, 159
flexibility, need for, 119, 188
Foster, Henry H., 151
Freed, Doris Jonas, 151
friends
    of deceased wives, 62–63
    of stepchild, 92–93
friendship, with stepchildren, 15, 188, 196, 230
funerals, 157

generosity, benefits and pitfalls, 142, 147–48
gift giving, holidays and, 134
good stepmother syndrome, 237–239
graduations, 159–60

grief, over wife/mother's death, 57–60, 194
guilt
    remarried husbands and, 26, 30–31, 35, 106, 142, 169, 170
    stepchildren and, 79, 208
    stepmothers and, 7, 20–24, 66–67, 116, 135, 223
    vacation issues and, 125–26, 129–30

half siblings, 18–19, 172–78, 241
Hallmark, 3
heirlooms, 64
holidays, 124, 127, 132–40
    ex-wives' inclusion at, 51–52
    gift giving, 134
    importance of planning for, 136–38
    mixed stepfamilies and, 189
    not getting together for, 139–40
homemaker/maid syndrome, 111–12
housekeeping issues, 108–13
humor, need for, 222
husbands, remarried, 25–40
    communication's importance with, 38–40, 119–22
    competition for attention and, 31–34
    conflicts with, 27–29
    custodial stepmothers and, 183–88, 191, 193–94
    ex-wives of. *See* ex-wives
    funerals for, 157
    guilt and, 26, 30–31, 35, 106, 125–26, 129–30, 142, 169, 170

stepmothers *(cont'd)*
ex-wives and. *See* ex-wives
family gatherings and, 155–63,
240
focusing on self by, 220–23
guilt and, 7, 20–24, 66–67, 116,
125–26, 135, 223
housekeeping issues and, 108–13
husband's funeral and, 157
isolation of, xv, 6–7
marital relationship concerns of,
34–37, 89–90, 114–27, 136,
222
never-before-married women as,
17, 33, 127
overinvolvement of, 224–26
as positive influence, 226–28
realistic model development by,
9
rewards and benefits for, 117–18,
228–31, 239–41
sexual intimacy issues of, 89–90
starting a new family by, 18–19,
164–80
stepchildren's reactions to, 71–
83
stepchild visits and, 84–98
stepfamily relations over time with,
232–42
stereotypical views of, 2, 3, 5–6,
18
vacation concerns of, 123–31

stepsiblings, 189–91, 241
support groups, 144, 214, 218–19

titles, to houses, 145
toddler stepchildren, 78

vacations, 123–31
Visher, Emily and John, 18, 78, 80,
92, 101–102, 126, 144, 198,
231
visits, from stepchildren, 84–98,
114–15, 120–21
children's self-defensiveness
during, 91–93
initial stays, 86–87
legal terms and conditions, 44–45,
93–94
long-distance stepmothering and,
94–97
parental intimacy issues and, 89–90
premarital discussion of, 120–21
vacations and, 123–31

weddings, 158–60, 240
widowers, 2, 57–65
deceased wife's belongings and,
63–65
friends of deceased wife and,
62–63
inheritance issues, 64–65
second wife's guilt and, 21
wills. *See* inheritance issues

About the Author

Cherie Burns is a freelance writer in New York City. She has worked as a journalist in Denver, San Francisco, Los Angeles, and New York. Her work has appeared in the *New York Times*, *People*, *Glamour*, *Sports Illustrated*, *Working Woman*, *New York*, *Constitution*, and *Us*. She has written for both film and television and has also worked in the publishing world as a literary agent. Her book, *Stepmotherhood: How to Survive Without Feeling Frustrated, Left Out, or Wicked* has sold over 40,000 copies both here and in Britain and Germany since it was originally published in 1986. One of the first writers to address step-family issues, the author speaks publicly to local and national stepfamily groups and organizations. She has been quoted in *Time, Fortune, People, American Health,* and *Glamour* and has made numerous television appearances.

Cherie is the mother of two children, Alex, 19, and Jessie, 17, stepmother to two adult stepdaughters, and stepgrandmother to two stepgrandchildren. She is married to the journalist Richard L. Duncan